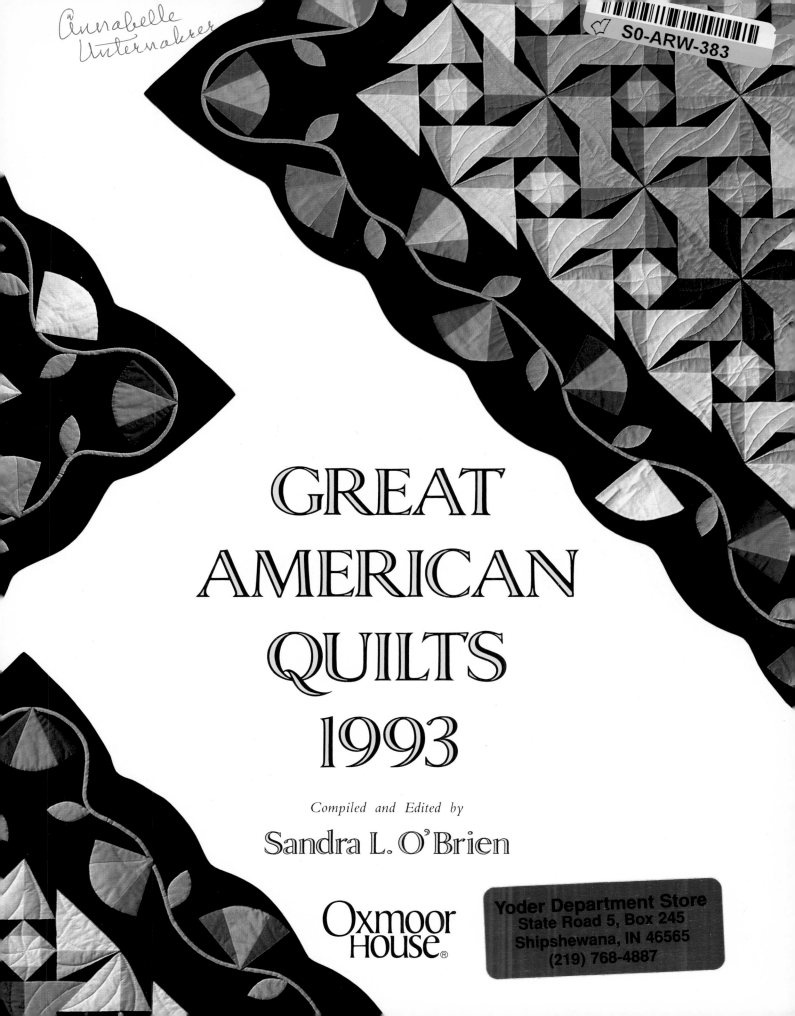

GREAT AMERICAN QUILTS 1993

Compiled and Edited by

Sandra L. O'Brien

Oxmoor House®

CONTENTS

Library of Congress Catalog Number: 86-62283
ISBN: 0-8487-1151-3
ISSN: 0890-8222
Manufactured in the United States of America
Fourth Printing 1993

Editor-in-Chief: Nancy J. Fitzpatrick
Senior Crafts Editor: Susan Ramey Wright
Senior Editor, Editorial Services: Olivia Wells
Director of Manufacturing: Jerry Higdon
Art Director: James Boone

Great American Quilts 1993

Editor: Sandra L. O'Brien
Editorial Assistant: Catherine S. Corbett
Copy Chief: Mary Jean Haddin
Assistant Copy Editor: Susan Smith Cheatham
Production Manager: Rick Litton
Associate Production Manager: Theresa L. Beste
Production Assistant: Pam Beasley Bullock
Designer: Melinda P. Goode
Patterns and Illustrations: Karen Tindall Tillery, Larry Hunter
Senior Photographer: John O'Hagan

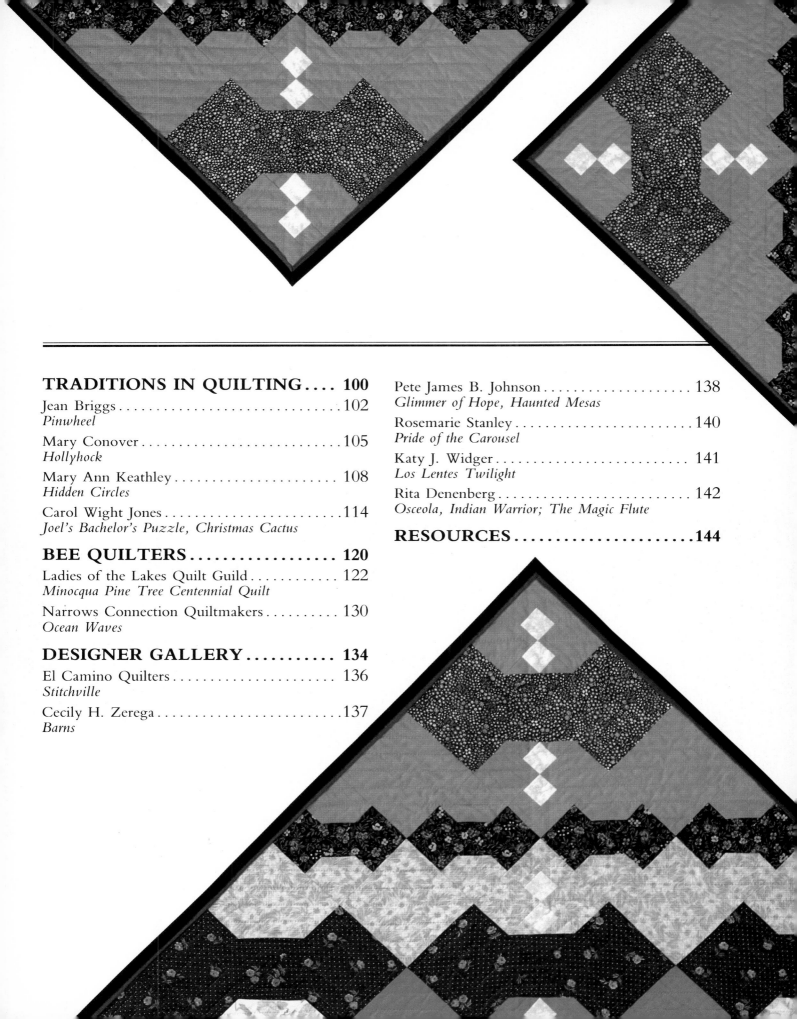

Basic Quiltmaking Techniques

Following is a brief guide for quiltmaking. The instructions for each quilt in this book contain the methods preferred by the particular quilter and may differ slightly from the techniques described here.

Preparing Fabric

To preshrink, wash, dry, and press all fabrics before cutting out pieces.

Enlarging a Pattern from a Grid

On all grids in this book, each square equals 1". That means you should draw an enlarging grid of 1" squares on graph paper or gridded freezer paper, which is already gridded with ⅛" or ¼" squares, or on plain paper. Copy the design freehand, one square at a time, from the gridded pattern to your enlarging grid.

Also, gridded patterns may be enlarged by using a photocopy machine. In this book, if the squares on the gridded pattern are ½", enlarge 200%; if the squares are ¾", enlarge 133%.

Making Templates

A template is a copy of a printed pattern that is used to mark the shape onto fabric. We recommend transparent template plastic, which is available at craft supply and quilt shops.

Trace the pattern piece onto the template plastic. For machine piecing, trace along outside solid (cutting) line. For hand piecing, trace along inside broken (stitching) line. Cut out template along traced line. Label each template with pattern name, letter, grain line arrow, and match points (corner dots). Punch a small hole in the template at each match point.

Marking and Cutting Fabric

Place template facedown on the wrong side of the fabric and mark around the template with a sharp pencil. Mark match points through punched holes. If using templates for hand piecing, leave at least ¾" between each template for seam allowances; cut out pieces, adding ¼" seam allowances. If using templates for machine piecing, cut out pieces on pencil line.

Hand Piecing

To hand piece, place two fabric pieces together with right sides facing and edges aligned. Insert pins at match points and at strategic places along seam line. Insert a threaded needle through both layers of fabric at the match point and take a few small running stitches along seam line. Then backstitch to secure the stitches. Continue stitching and backstitching every few stitches to secure. Check your stitching as you go to be sure that you are stitching in the seam line of both pieces. Stitch from match point to match point. Do not stitch into seam allowances. Press seam allowances to one side, usually toward the darker fabric.

Never sew across seam allowances when joining patches. Instead, insert needle through both layers of fabric at match point of one patch and bring it up through match point of other patch. This allows a free-floating seam allowance that can be pressed in either direction.

Machine Piecing

To machine piece, place two fabric pieces together with right sides facing and edges aligned. Insert pins at match points and at strategic places along seam line. Do not stitch over pins but remove them before reaching the needle.

Use a presser foot that gives a perfect ¼" seam allowance by aligning the raw edge of the fabric with the outside edge of the presser foot. If you have no such presser foot, measure ¼" from the sewing-machine needle to a point on the throat plate and mark that point with a strip of masking tape.

Stitch from raw edge to raw edge. It is not necessary to backstitch at the beginning and end of seams because the stitching will be crossed by other lines of stitching.

Press seam allowances toward darker fabric. When joining blocks or rows, press the seam allowances of the top piece in one direction and the seam allowances of the bottom piece in the opposite direction. This method will help ensure that seam allowances lie flat.

Stitching Curved Seams

To sew curves, first fold both concave and convex pieces in half to locate and mark the center (Stitching Curves Diagram I). Place the two pieces with right sides facing and with the concave piece on top. Match the center marks and pin at that point. Then match the edges at which the seam will begin and pin them. Curving the concave edge to align the raw edges, pin the pieces as needed in the interval between the two pins, as shown in Diagram II. Match and pin the edges where the seam will end and place pins between them and the center in the same manner (Diagram III). With the concave piece on top, stitch the seam slowly, removing the pins just before the needle reaches them. Do not sew over pins.

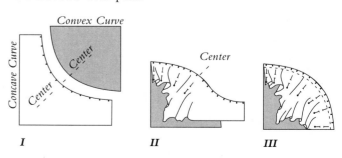

Stitching Curves Diagrams

Machine Appliquéing

Method 1. Cut pieces without seam allowances. Fuse the finished-size appliqué piece to the background fabric with lightweight fusible or paper-backed fusible webbing. This stabilizes the piece on the background and makes machine stitching easier. Cover raw edges with a medium-width satin stitch.

Method 2. Cut pieces without seam allowances. Apply a piece of lightweight fusible interfacing to the finished-size piece. Anchor the piece to the background using a glue stick. Cover raw edges with a satin stitch.

Method 3. Cut pieces with seam allowances. Anchor the piece to the background fabric by machine-basting on the seam line. Trim the excess appliqué fabric outside the seam line. Cover basting with a satin stitch.

Hand Appliquéing

Hand appliqué is the best way to achieve the look of traditional appliqué. However, using freezer paper, which is sold in the grocery store, can save a lot of time because it eliminates the need for hand basting the seam allowances.

Make templates without seam allowances. Mark around the template onto the dull side of the freezer paper and cut the paper on the marked line. Make a freezer paper shape for each piece to be appliquéd. Pin the freezer paper shape, with its shiny side up, to the wrong side of your fabric. Following the paper shape and adding a scant ¼" seam allowance, cut out the fabric piece. Do not remove the pins. Use the tip of a hot, dry iron to press the seam allowance to the shiny side of the freezer paper. Do not touch the shiny side of the freezer paper with the iron. Remove the pins.

Pin the appliqué shape in place on the background fabric. Use one strand of sewing thread in a color to match the appliqué shape. Using small slipstitches or blindstitches, appliqué the shape to the background.

After stitching is complete, cut away the background fabric behind the appliqué shape, leaving ¼" seam allowance. Separate the freezer paper from the fabric with your fingernail and pull gently to remove it.

Mitering Borders

To miter borders, first measure your quilt. Cut two borders to fit the shorter of the two opposite sides, plus the width of the border plus 2". Center the measurement for the shorter side on one border and place a pin at each end of the measurement. Match the pins on the border to the corners of the longer side of the quilt. Join the border to the quilt, easing the quilt to fit between the pins and stopping ¼" from each corner. Join the remaining cut border to the opposite side of the quilt. Cut and join the remaining borders in the same manner. Press seams to one side. Follow Mitered Borders Diagrams I through III to miter corners.

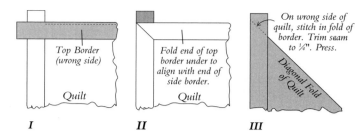

Mitered Borders Diagrams

Marking Your Quilt Top

After the quilt top is completed, press it and mark it with quilting designs. The most popular methods for marking involve using stencils or templates. Both can be purchased, or you can make your own. Use a #2 lead pencil for marking light to medium fabrics and a white artist's pencil on dark fabrics.

Making a Backing

While some fabric and quilt shops sell 90" and 108" widths of backing fabric, the instructions in *Great American Quilts* always give backing yardage based on 45"-wide fabric. When using 45"-wide fabric, all quilts wider than 42" will require a pieced backing. For quilts whose width measures between 42" and 80", purchase an amount of fabric equal to two times the desired length of the unfinished quilt backing. (The unfinished quilt backing should be at least 3" larger on all sides than the quilt top.)

The backing fabric should be of a type and color that is compatible with the quilt top. Percale sheets are not recommended because they are tightly woven and difficult to hand-quilt through.

A pieced backing for a bed quilt should have three panels. The three-panel backing is recommended because it tends to wear better and lie flatter than the two-panel type, whose seam often makes a ridge down the center of the quilt.

Begin by cutting the fabric in half widthwise (see Quilt Backing Diagram I). Open the two lengths and stack them, with right sides facing and selvages aligned. Stitch along both selvage edges to create a tube of fabric (Diagram II). Cut down the center of the top layer of fabric only and open the fabric flat (Diagram III).

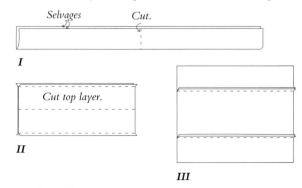

Quilt Backing Diagrams

Layering and Basting

After the quilt top and backing are made, the next steps are layering and basting in preparation for quilting. Prepare a large working surface to spread out the quilt—a large table, two tables pushed together, or the floor. Place the backing on the working surface wrong side up. Unfold the batting and place it on top of the backing. Smooth any wrinkles or lumps in the batting. Lay the quilt top wrong side down on top of the batting and backing. Make sure the backing and quilt top are aligned. Knot a long strand of sewing thread and use a darning needle for basting. Begin basting in the center of your quilt and baste out toward the edges. The stitches should cover an ample amount of the quilt so that the quilt layers do not shift during quilting. Inadequate basting can result in puckers and folds on the back and front of the quilt.

Hand Quilting

Hand quilting can be done with the quilt in a hoop or in a floor frame. It is best to start quilting in the middle of your quilt and work out toward the edges.

Most quilters use a very thin, short needle called a "between." Betweens are available in sizes 7 to 12, with 7 being the longest and 12 the shortest. If you are a beginning quilter, try a size 7 or 8; because betweens are so much shorter than other hand-sewing needles, they may feel awkward at first.

To begin, thread your needle with an 18" to 24" length of quilting thread and make a small knot at one end. Insert the needle into the top of the quilt approximately ½" from the point you want to begin quilting. Do not take the needle through all three layers, but stop it in the batting and bring it up through the quilt top again at your starting point. Tug gently on the thread to pop the knot through the quilt top into the batting. This anchors the thread without an unsightly knot showing on the back. With your non-sewing hand underneath the quilt, insert the needle straight down in the quilt about 1/16" from the starting point. (See Hand Quilting Diagram I.) With your underneath finger, feel for the point as the needle comes through the backing. Place the thumb of your sewing hand approximately ½" ahead of your needle. At the moment you feel the needle touch your underneath finger, push the fabric up from below as you rock the needle down to a nearly horizontal position. Using the thumb of your sewing hand in conjunction with the underneath hand, pinch a little hill in the fabric and push the tip of the needle through the quilt top. (See Diagram II.)

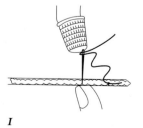   

I   *II*

Hand Quilting Diagrams

Now either push the needle all the way through to complete one stitch or rock the needle again to an upright position on its point to take another stitch. Take no more than a quarter-needleful of stitches before pulling the needle through.

When you have about 6" of thread remaining, you must end the old thread securely and invisibly. Carefully tie a knot in the thread, flat against the surface of the fabric. Pop the knot through the top as you did when beginning the line of quilting. Clip the thread, rethread your needle, and continue quilting.

Machine Quilting

Quilting by machine is as old as the sewing machine itself; but until recently, it was thought inferior to hand quilting. To see just how beautiful machine quilting can be, see Debra Wagner's *Winter Bouquet* quilt on page 90.

Machine quilting can be done on your sewing machine using a straight, even stitch and special presser feet. There are two commonly used types of machine quilting: straight line and free motion. A walking foot, or even-feed foot, is required for straight-line machine quilting to help the top fabric move through the machine at the same rate that the feed dogs move the bottom fabric. A darning foot is used with free-motion machine quilting to protect your fingers and to prevent skipped stitches. Nylon thread or regular sewing thread can be used for machine quilting.

Baste your quilt layers together with brass safety pins, since thread-basting will catch in the presser foot. Place pins at 4" intervals and fasten them on the top of the quilt. Remove the pins as you quilt.

With the quilt top facing you, roll the long edges of the quilt toward the center of the quilt, leaving a 12"-wide area unrolled in the center. Secure the rolls with bicycle clips, metal bands that are available at quilt shops. Begin at one unrolled end and fold the quilt over and over until only a small area is showing. This will be the area where you will begin to machine quilt.

Place the folded portion of the quilt in your lap. Start machine quilting in the center and work to the right side of the quilt, unfolding and unrolling the quilt as you go. Remove the quilt from the machine, turn it, and reinsert it in the machine to stitch the left side. A table placed behind your sewing machine will help support the quilt as it is stitched. Always stop with the needle down to keep the quilt from shifting.

Curves and circles are made by free-motion machine quilting. Using a darning foot and with feed dogs down, the quilt is moved under the needle by the slight movement of your fingertips. Place your fingertips on the fabric on each side of the presser foot and run your machine at a steady, medium speed. The length of the stitches is determined by the rate of speed at which you move the fabric through the machine. Do not rotate the quilt; rather, move it from side to side as needed. Always stop with the needle down to keep the quilt from shifting.

Machine stippling is a form of free-motion machine quilting. Curved lines of machine stitching are spaced very closely without crossing. The density of the quilting gives that area of the quilt texture and causes it to flatten, while the unquilted areas around it seem to be raised up.

Making Binding

A continuous bias strip is frequently used by quilters for all kinds of quilts but is especially recommended for those with curved edges. Follow these steps to make a continuous bias strip:

1. To make continuous bias binding, you'll need a square of fabric. Multiply the number of inches of binding needed by the desired width of the binding (usually 2½"). Use a calculator to find the square root of that number. That's the size of the square needed to make your binding.

2. Cut the square in half diagonally.

3. With right sides facing and raw edges aligned, join triangles to form a sawtooth, as shown in Continuous Bias Binding Diagram I.

4. Open sawtooth and press seam of parallelogram open. Mark off parallel lines the desired width of the binding, as shown in Diagram II below.

5. With right sides facing, align the raw edges marked Seam 2. As you align the edges, extend a Seam 2 point past its natural matching point by the distance of the width of the bias strip and join.

6. Cut the binding in a continuous strip, starting with the protruding point and following the marked lines around the tube. (See Diagram III.)

7. Press the binding strip in half lengthwise, with wrong sides facing. This gives you double-fold, or French, binding, which is sturdier than single-fold binding.

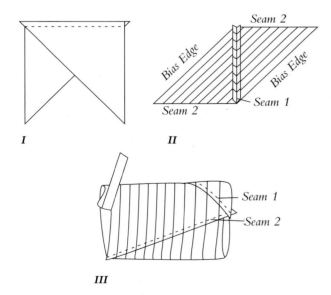

Continuous Bias Binding Diagrams

Attaching Binding

To prepare your quilt for binding, stitch layers together by stitching ¼" from quilt edge. Trim excess batting and backing. Place the binding on the quilt top with right sides facing and raw edges aligned. Start stitching at the midpoint of one side of your quilt. Backstitch at the beginning and end of stitching. Stitch through all layers, mitering the corners.

Trapunto

Trapunto is a stuffing method that raises selected areas of the quilt top to create an added dimension. There are two basic methods for stuffing in quiltmaking: the **backing method** or the **lining method**. With the backing method, stuffing is inserted between the threads of the quilt's backing after the quilt has been layered. When an instrument is inserted into the quilt's backing, it misaligns fabric threads that often cannot be repaired. Therefore, the lining method is favored by many quilters because the stuffing is inserted before the quilt is layered. (*Winter Bouquet* on page 90 uses a machine-stitched backing method.) Follow the guidelines below for using the lining method:

1. After marking the trapunto design on the quilt top, cut a piece of batiste or other loosely woven lightweight fabric equal to the size of the area for stuffing. Use this as the lining and baste it to the wrong side of your quilt top. Avoid placing basting stitches in areas where trapunto will be worked.

2. Place the basted fabrics in a small embroidery hoop. Using two strands of embroidery floss, backstitch along all trapunto lines.

3. Turn the work to the back and cut a small slit in the lining. Using an orange stick, push small amounts of stuffing through the slit up against the embroidered line. Continue stuffing until the area is full and firm.

4. Close the opening with loose stitches to secure the stuffing. The quilt top is now ready for quilting.

Rules of Thumb

All pattern pieces in this book include ¼" seam allowances. All measurements for pieces, sashing, and borders include seam allowances, unless otherwise noted. Some oversize pieces are placed on grids, with scale information noted. (See page 4 for information on enlarging a pattern.)

Fabric requirements are based on 44/45"-wide fabric with trimmed selvages, and requirements for backing on bed quilts are based on a three-panel backing. *Generous allowances are given for fabric requirements to account for fabric shrinkage and individual differences in cutting.* Fabric requirements are given for one-piece borders. The finished quilt size is the size of the quilt before quilting.

FABULOUS
FANS

Mary Ann Keathley

Jacksonville, Arkansas

Since piecing her first quilt top as a young girl, Mary has maintained a lifelong faithfulness to all kinds of needlework. "I am happiest when I have a needle in my hand," says Mary. "Quilting has been my salvation, especially since my retirement. I enjoy it tremendously."

Mary gains most of her inspiration for quilt designs from antique quilts and is particularly fond of scrap quilts. Both *Mary's Fan*, shown on this page, and *Hidden Circles*, in "Traditions in Quilting," are variations of antique quilts using fabric scraps. Most of the time, the greatest challenge in this type of quiltmaking is drafting the patterns, since templates or printed patterns are often unavailable. We applaud Mary for her dedication to this technique.

Mary's Fan
1990
Inspired by an antique quilt of Grandmother's Fans set in this arrangement, Mary was delighted to find a quilt design in which she could use her scraps. Fabric scraps are used for the fans, and loads of feather quilting embrace each one. The top is completely machine-pieced, and Mary assures us that it is easy to make!

Mary's Fan

Finished Quilt Size
92" x 92"

Number of Blocks and Finished Size
64 blocks—11½" x 11½"

Fabric Requirements
Dk. green print   —2¾ yd.★
Scraps   —5¾ yd. total
Muslin   —5¾ yd.
Backing   —8 yd.
★Includes yardage for bias binding.

Other Materials
Green quilting thread

Number to Cut
Template A   —64 dk. green print
Template B   —448 scraps
Template C   —64 muslin

Quilt Top Assembly
1. Join 7 fan blades (B), as shown in Block Piecing Diagram. Join pieces A and C to bottom and top of fan blades, as shown. Make 64 blocks.
2. Arrange blocks in 8 rows of 8 blocks each, as shown in Setting Diagram. Lay out all blocks before joining them to make sure that they are positioned correctly. (Note that top half of quilt is a mirror image of bottom half.) Stack blocks in rows and label each row.

   Join blocks at sides to form rows and join rows.

Quilting
Quilt in-the-ditch of fan blade seams. Quilt Mary's feather quilting pattern, using green quilting thread in muslin pieces (C).

Finished Edges
Bind with dk. green print.

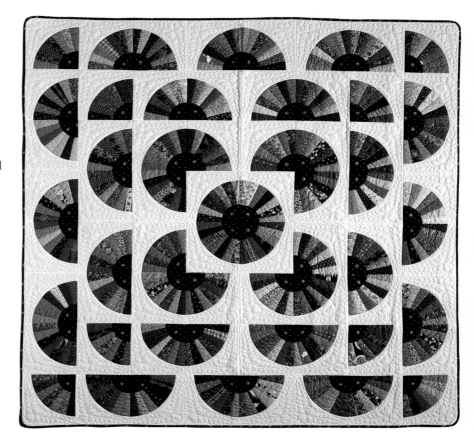

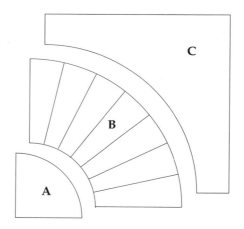

Block Piecing Diagram

Setting Diagram

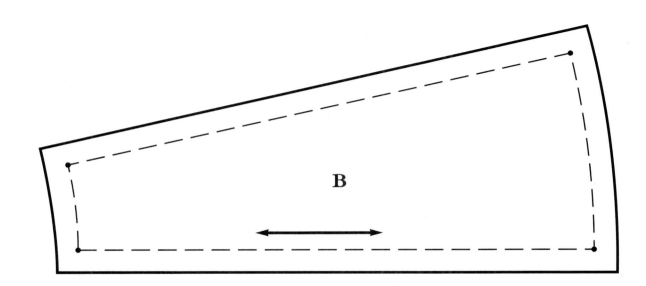

B

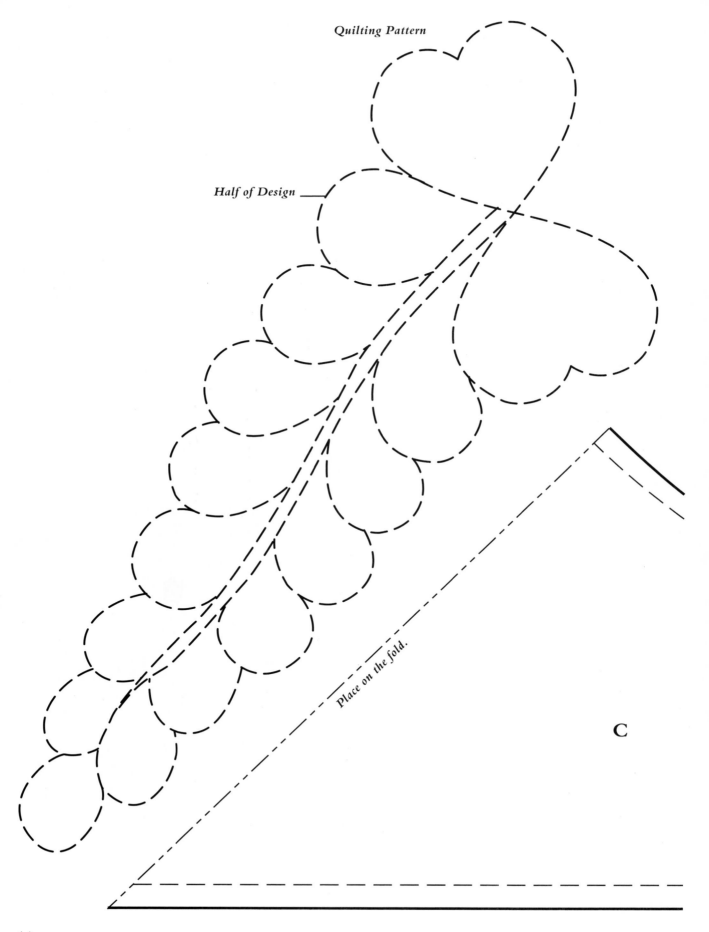

Quilting Pattern

Half of Design

Place on the fold.

C

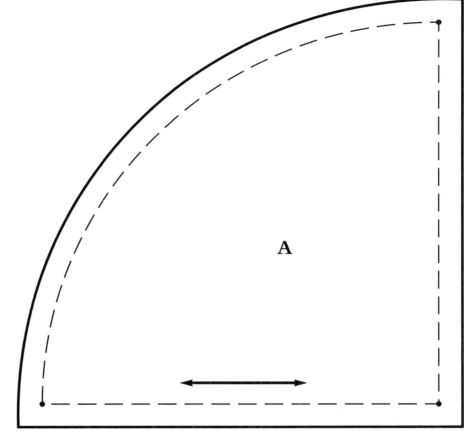

A

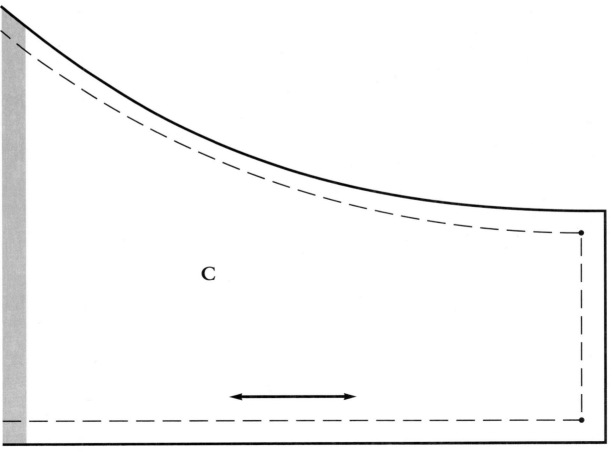

C

Shaded portion indicates overlap from preceding page.

Sheri Wilkinson Lalk

Electra, Texas

Sheri Wilkinson Lalk has been making quilts for the last 15 years and doesn't intend to stop. "I have a need to create things," she says, "and quilting is the medium that allows me to express myself best." Sheri likes to use all kinds of quilting techniques and patterns, but her favorite segment of quiltmaking is to take a traditional pattern and spin off an original design or setting.

Being a member of the Red River Quilters' Guild of Wichita Falls, Texas, is an important facet of Sheri's quilting. "I have made so many new friends through the guild," she says. "I find that quilters are always generous with their knowledge and even with their supplies."

In "Quilts Across America," you'll find Sheri's version of a compass quilt, *Starlight Compass*.

Jacob's Fan and Flowers
1990

Blissfully flowered vines dance among a convergence of widespread fans in Sheri's symmetrical design. The successful juxtaposing of blocks with opposite styles, such as the geometrics of Jacob's Ladder and the curves of Grandmother's Fan, is difficult at best, but Sheri shows us how to organize them to exude both rhythm and eye-appeal.

Template Q — 96 white print#
96 striped print
Template R — 16 lavender print
Template S — 16 med. pink print★★
80 misc. pink prints
Template T — 16 white print#
Template U — 2 med. pink print
★★See step 7 before cutting fabric.
★★★See step 2 before cutting fabric.
#See step 1 before cutting fabric.

Quilt Top Assembly

1. Cut one 24½" square and twelve 12½" squares from white print.

Finger-press 24½" square in half diagonally in both directions to form guidelines. Position template K (circle) in center of square and use it to lightly mark matchpoints and circle outline for additional guidelines.

Arrange pieces A through J on square, as shown in Placement Diagram I. Layer-appliqué pieces in place. (Numbers in parentheses in Placement Diagram I indicate order for appliquéing.)

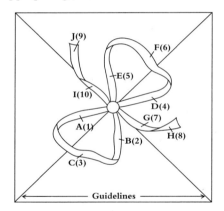

Placement Diagram I

2. Make 11½ yards of ¾"-wide bias from green pindot for stems. Pin stems, flowers, and leaves to square, as shown in Placement Diagram II.

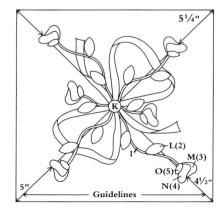

Placement Diagram II

Jacob's Fan and Flowers

Finished Quilt Size
76" x 100"

Number of Blocks and Finished Size
16 Grandmother's
Fan blocks—12" x 12"
16 Jacob's Ladder
blocks—12" x 12"

Fabric Requirements
Med. pink print — 3¼ yd.
Lt. pink print — ½ yd.
Misc. pink prints — 1⅜ yd. total
Lavender print — 1 yd.
Purple print — ¼ yd.
White print — 3¼ yd.
Striped print — 1 yd.
Green pindot — 2 yd.★
Med. pink print for
bias binding — 1¼ yd.

Backing — 5⅞ yd.
★Set aside 1¼ yd. for bias strips for stems.

Number to Cut
Template A — 1 med. pink print★★
Template B — 1 med. pink print★★
Template C — 1 lt. pink print
Template D — 1 med. pink print★★
Template E — 1 med. pink print★★
Template F — 1 lt. pink print
Template G — 1 lt. pink print
Template H — 1 med. pink print★★
Template I — 1 lt. pink print
Template J — 1 med. pink print★★
Template K — 1 lt. pink print
Template L — 74 green pindot★★★
Template M — 30 purple print
Template N — 30 lavender print
Template O — 30 green pindot★★★
Template P — 96 lavender print
96 white print#

Layer-appliqué pieces in order shown. Appliqué bow knot (K) last.

3. Join squares (P) and triangles (Q), as shown in Jacob's Ladder Block Piecing Diagram and quilt photograph. Make 16 blocks.

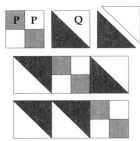

Jacob's Ladder Block Piecing Diagram

4. Join 6 fan blades (S), as shown in Grandmother's Fan Block Piecing Diagram. Include a med. pink print piece (S) in each fan. (See quilt photograph.)

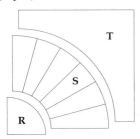

*Grandmother's Fan
Block Piecing Diagram*

Join fan to pieces R and T to complete block. Make 16 blocks.

5. Join Grandmother's Fan blocks, Jacob's Ladder blocks, and white print squares in 6 rows of 6 blocks each, as shown in Setting Diagram I.

Join 4 Grandmother's Fan blocks and 4 Jacob's Ladder blocks to 24½" appliquéd square to make center section, as shown in Setting Diagrams I and II.

Join rows to center section, as shown.

6. Arrange trailing vines on white print squares, as shown in quilt photograph, and appliqué in place. Layer-appliqué leaves, flowers, and hearts (U).

7. Cut 2 borders, 2½" wide, from med. pink print. Join to opposite sides of quilt.

Cut 2 borders, 2½" wide, from med. pink print. Join to top and bottom of quilt.

Quilting
Outline-quilt outside seam lines of all appliquéd pieces. Outline-quilt ¼" inside seam lines of all patchwork.

Finished Edges
Bind with med. pink print.

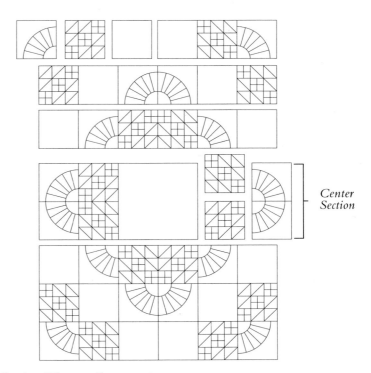

*Center
Section*

Setting Diagram I

Setting Diagram II

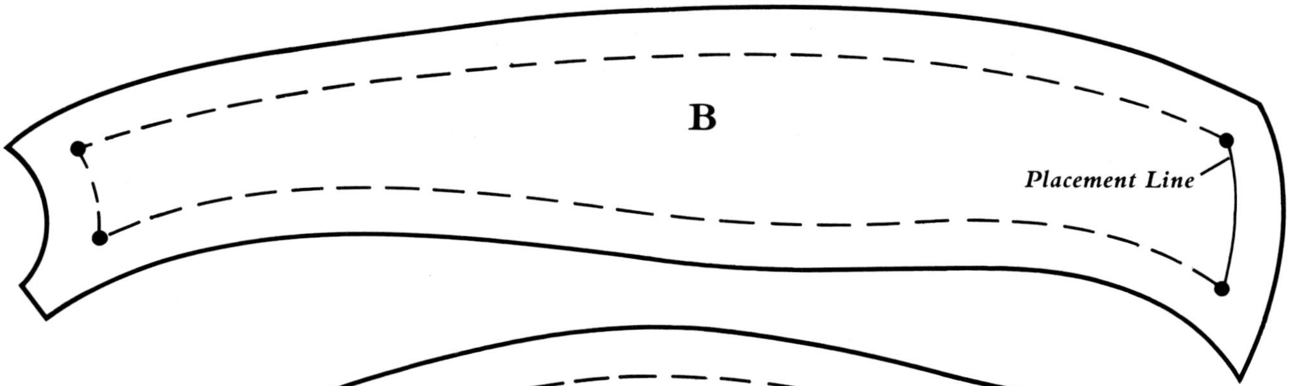

B

Placement Line

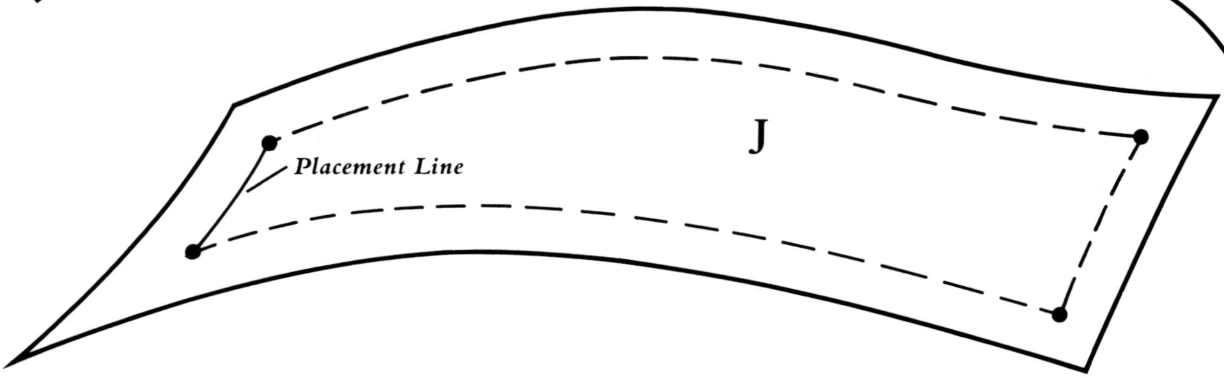

J

Placement Line

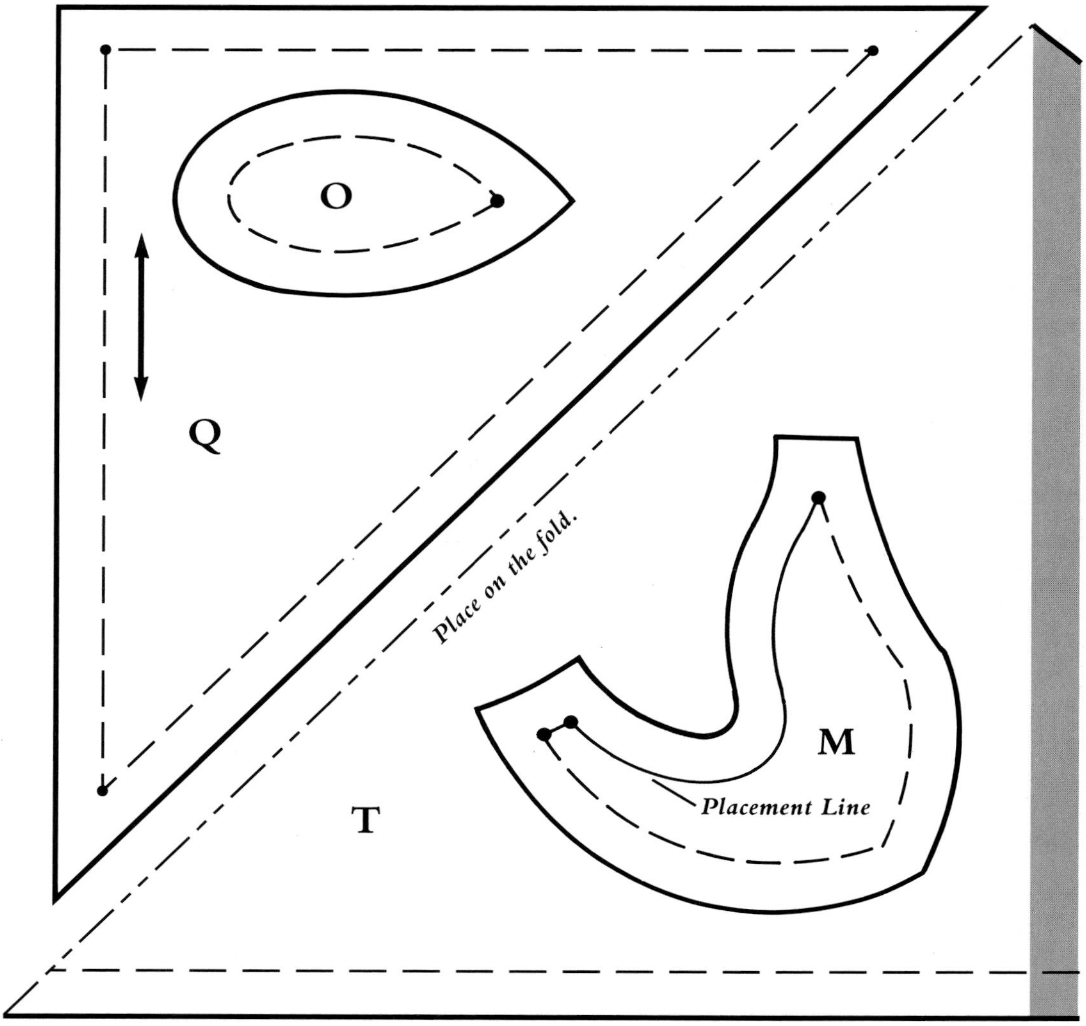

O

Q

T

Place on the fold.

M

Placement Line

Shaded portion indicates overlap from following page.

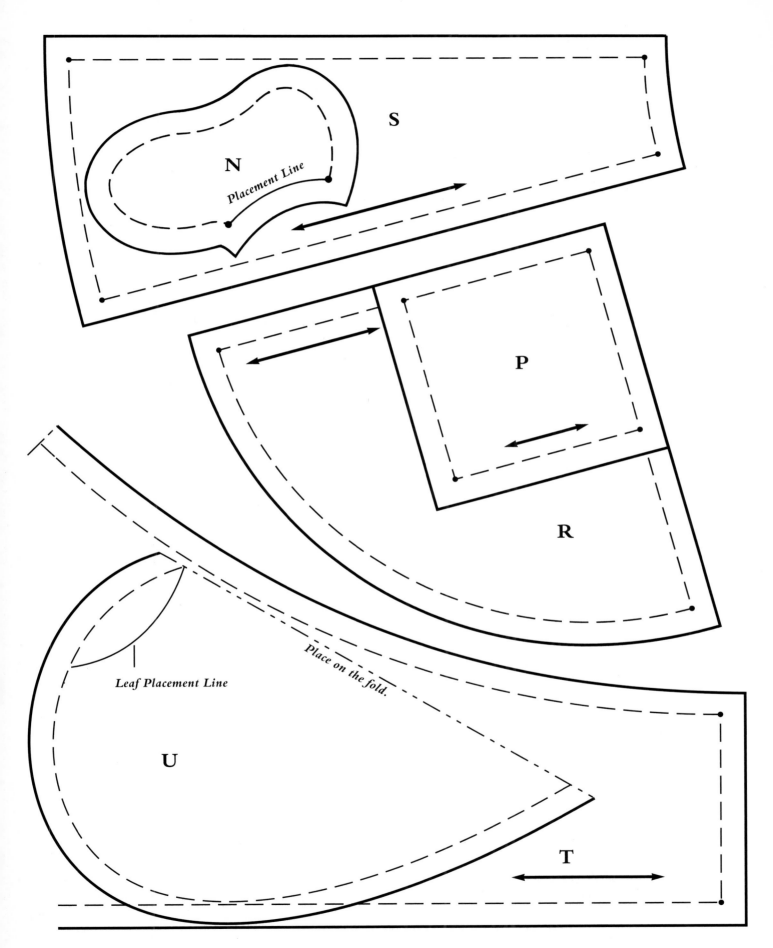

N

S

Placement Line

P

R

Leaf Placement Line

Place on the fold.

U

T

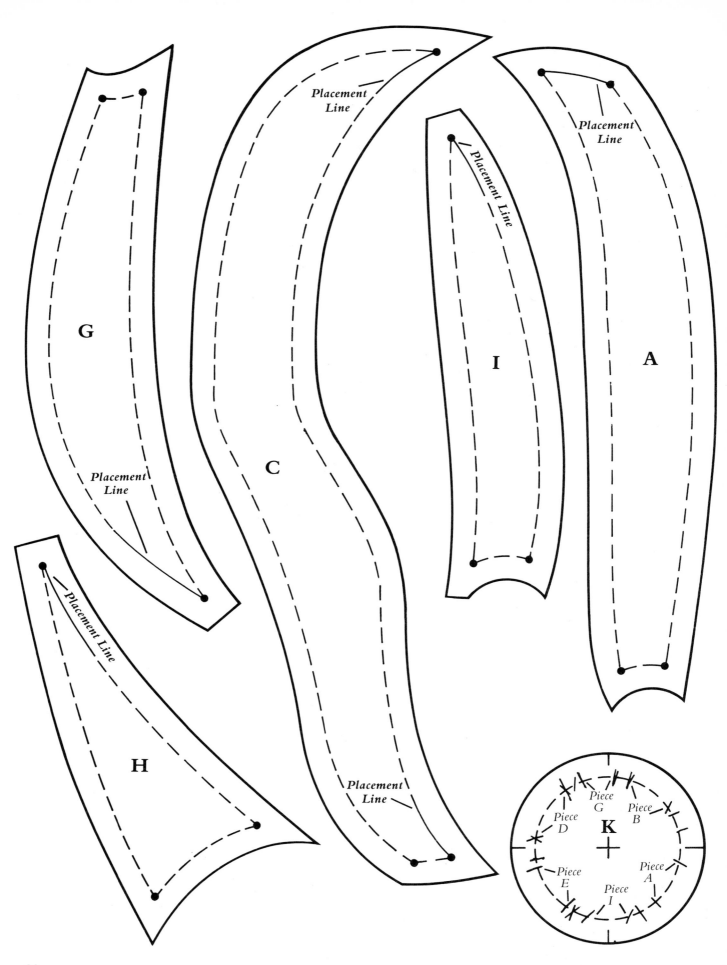

Placement Line

Placement Line

Placement Line

Placement Line

G

C

I

A

Placement Line

Placement Line

H

Placement Line

Piece G

Piece B

Piece D

K

Piece E

Piece A

Piece I

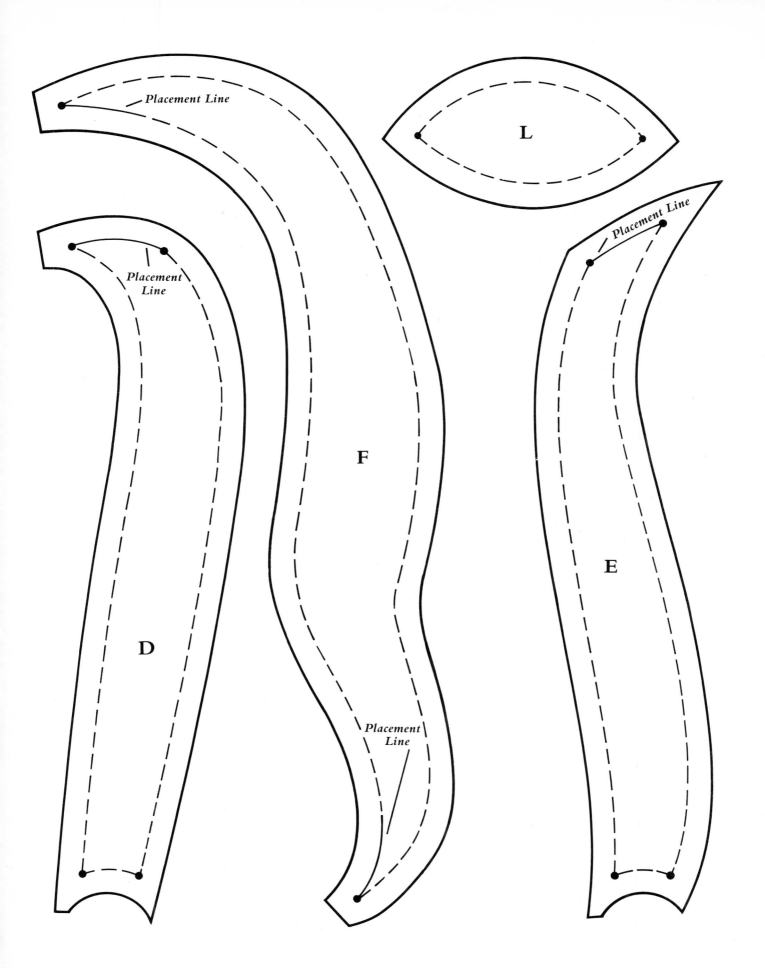

Placement Line

L

Placement Line

Placement Line

F

D

E

Placement Line

23

Jeanne Benson

Columbia, Maryland

This professional artist and quilter has been recognized nationally and internationally for her contributions to the fiber arts. Her works have been displayed in such places as the American Embassy in Monrovia, Liberia, as well as the juried Quilt San Diego exhibit. She is an artist in residence at the Montpelier Cultural Arts Center in Laurel, Maryland, where she conducts workshops, lectures for the public as well as for the Resident Associate Program of the Smithsonian Institution.

She began quilting 14 years ago when she became fascinated with the block designs she had seen in sampler quilts. It is not surprising that she enjoys the design phase of quiltmaking most. "Setting up a problem for myself, working through my ideas, and coming to a solution are my favorite parts," says Jeanne.

Jeanne also shares with us her simple method for making a fabric collage keepsake in our "Quilts Across America."

Emily's Quilt
1987

When Jeanne made this quilt, her daughter Emily was five years old. Says Jeanne, "I made this quilt for my daughter, who is growing, changing, opening like the fan to herself and to me."

Jeanne expertly combined machine and hand quilting to enhance each facet of *Emily's Quilt*. Satin-stitched ribbons "dangle" from each fan, and every fan is smartly framed using Jeanne's well-known skewed Log Cabin technique. (See "Resources.") The random-pieced Seminole border offers a chance for quilters to have fun with their rotary cutters. And last, but not least, Jeanne embellished her quilt with two small fabric dolls.

It is no surprise that *Emily's Quilt* has won a few ribbons. In 1988 it was awarded the Best Creative Use of a Traditional Design ribbon at Quilts of Merit, Woodlawn Plantation, Mount Vernon, Virginia; and a second place ribbon in the innovative pieced category at the Quilters' Heritage Celebration, Lancaster, Pennsylvania.

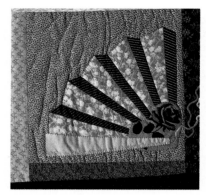

Emily's Quilt

Finished Quilt Size
61½" x 89½"

Number of Blocks and Finished Size
15 blocks—14" x 14"

Fabric Requirements

Gray print★	—1½ yd.
Black/white pinstripe	—2 yd.
Misc. prints★★	—½ yd. each
Gray with rose print	—⅜ yd
Lt. gray	—⅜ yd.
Lt. gray prints★★★	—½ yd. each
Black prints★★★	—½ yd. each
Dk. green print★★★★	—1 yd.
Green print★★★★	—1 yd.
Lt. green print#	—3¾ yd.
Lt. green for binding	—2½ yd.
Backing	—5½ yd.

★For block background
★★Select 15 prints, 1 for each fan.
★★★Select 4 prints for framing strips.
★★★★For pieced border
#For pieced border and outer border

Other Materials
Machine embroidery threads, variegated and solids
Black quilting thread
Green quilting thread

Number to Cut

Template A	—1 from each fan fabric
Template B	—15 black/white pinstripe##
Template C	—1 from each fan fabric
Template D	—15 black/white pinstripe##
Template E	—1 from each fan fabric
Template F	—15 black/white pinstripe##
Template G	—1 from each fan fabric
Template H	—15 black/white pinstripe##
Template I	—1 from each fan fabric
Template J	—15 black/white pinstripe##
Template K	—15 gray with rose print###
Template L	—15 lt. gray

##Cut pieces with stripes running across piece. See block photograph.
###Center rose in each heart.

Quilt Top Assembly
1. Join fan blades (A through J), as shown in Fan Piecing Diagram I and block photograph. (Use a single print for each fan.) Make 15 fans.
2. Cut fifteen 12" background squares from gray print. Lightly pencil a 10½" square on background square. Position each fan ½" inside pencil line of lower right corner of square and appliqué.
3. Appliqué hearts (K) to fans and squares, as shown in Fan Piecing Diagram II.

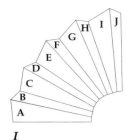
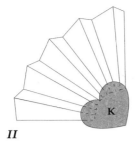
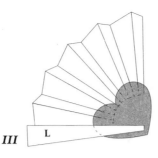

I   II   III

Fan Piecing Diagrams

4. Appliqué pieces (L) to fans and squares, as shown in Fan Piecing Diagram III.

Check placement of fan. "Sometimes appliqués 'move' on the background," says Jeanne, "and the extra fabric allows me to square up design." Trim squares to make 10½" squares.

5. Cut across lt. gray prints and black prints for framing strips to make 2¼"-wide strips.

Using Log Cabin piecing technique, join 1 round of strips to each fan square, as shown in Skewed Log Cabin Frame Diagram I. (Strips 2 and 3 are lt. gray print strips and strips 1 and 4, black print strips. See block photograph.)

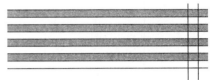

Skewed Log Cabin Frame Diagrams

Begin with a black print strip joined to bottom of square and join strips in a clockwise direction, as shown. Stop after fourth strip is joined.

Measure and mark 1½" from square seam line across framing strip 1 at left and 1" at right, as shown in Diagram II. Connect marks, drawing a line over framing strips at an angle. Trim along line. Join a black print framing strip to new edge.

Repeat for remaining sides, as shown in Diagram III.

When round 2 strips have been joined, trim framing strips to make a 14½" block. (See Diagram IV.) Repeat for each square to make 15 blocks.

6. Machine satin-stitch ribbon streamers on each fan, using variegated thread. (See block photograph.) Satin stitch width varies, but average width is ⅛".

7. Arrange fan blocks in 5 rows of 3 blocks each. Join blocks at sides to form rows and join rows.

8. Set aside 2¾ yd. of lt. green print for outer borders.

Fold and press ½ yd. of each fabric (dk. green print, green print, and lt. green print) for pieced borders in fourths. (See Border Piecing Diagram I.) Cut across folded fabrics at random angles to form wedges. Wedges

should be cut wide enough to include seam allowances so that finished pieces do not come to a point. (See pieces after joining in Diagram II.) Cut wedges at fold lines.

Alternate fabric wedges and join wedges to form units of 4 wedges each, as shown in Diagram II.

Cut across units at angles to make segments, as shown in Diagram III. (Again, cut segments wide enough to include seam allowances so that finished pieces do not come to a point.) Repeat until all wedges have been joined and segments cut.

Alternate segments in random manner and join in sets of 2, 3, or 4, as shown in Diagram IV. (Leave a few segments as singles.) Trim long edges of each set even.

9. Fold and press remaining ½ yd. of fabrics for pieced borders into fourths. Cut ¾"-wide strips across fabrics. Do not cut strips at folds.

Alternate fabrics and join strips lengthwise to form a panel, as shown in Stripped Panel Diagram.

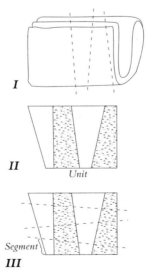

Border Piecing Diagrams

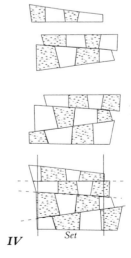

Stripped Panel Diagram

10. To make pieced borders for opposite sides of quilt, spread quilt on flat surface. Randomly arrange sets made in step 8 on opposite sides of quilt. Cut strips across seam lines of strip panel, made in step 9. Cut strips at various widths to insert between sets, either vertically or horizontally. (See photograph of border.)

Join sets and strips to form 2 long strips for side borders. Trim long edges even so that each strip is 3½"-wide. Join borders to sides of quilt.

Repeat for top and bottom of quilt.
11. Cut 2 borders, 7¼" wide, from lt. green print for sides of quilt. Join to quilt.

Cut 2 borders, 7¼" wide, from lt. green for top and bottom of quilt. Join to quilt.

Quilting

Jeanne recommends using a 100% cotton batting for machine quilting because the fabric sticks to it somewhat when it is pressed. After layering quilt, press quilt.

Start machine-quilting at center block and work your way toward quilt edges. Quilt in-the-ditch of all straight seam lines in Fan blocks (fan blades and framing strips). Pin-baste only along seam line to be machine-quilted. Stop after each line of stitching, pull threads to back, and tie off. "By tying off as you sew," says Jeanne, "you will avoid getting those threads caught in other stitching." After each line of stitching is complete, Jeanne presses

over the stitching on front and back. (Pressing on back assures that you have not made any unwanted pleats.)

Quilt in-the-ditch of all seams that run across pieced borders.

Outline-quilt by hand inside seam lines of fan outline, heart, and fan piece (L) with black quilting thread. Quilt straight and curving lines across outer border at varied intervals with green quilting thread.

Finished Edges

Jeanne likes the look of a narrow binding and cuts her straight-of-grain binding strips, 1½" wide, from lt. green. Before binding is turned to the back, it is pressed over the binding seam. It is folded onto itself and blindstitched to backing.

Embellishments

Jeanne appliquéd 2 fabric Japanese dolls to the border.

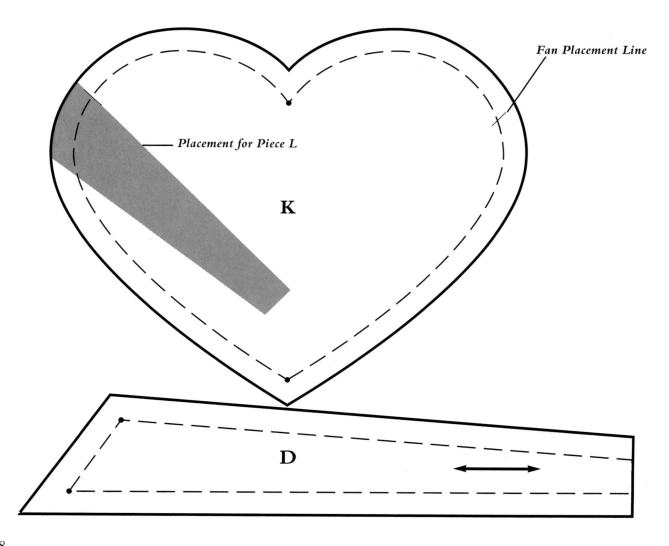

Fan Placement Line

Placement for Piece L

K

D

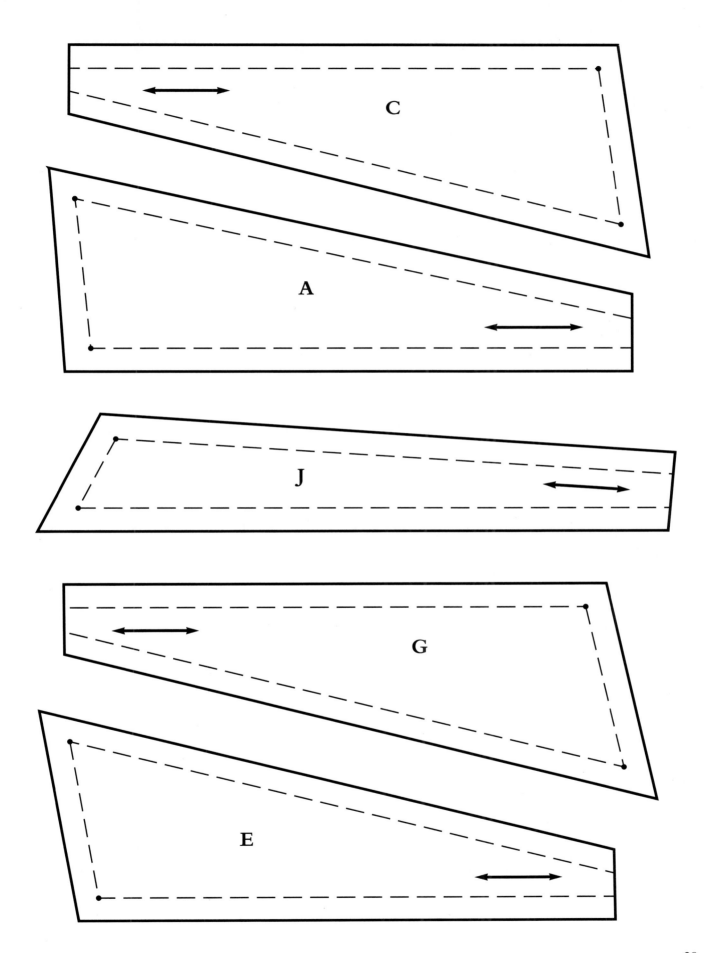

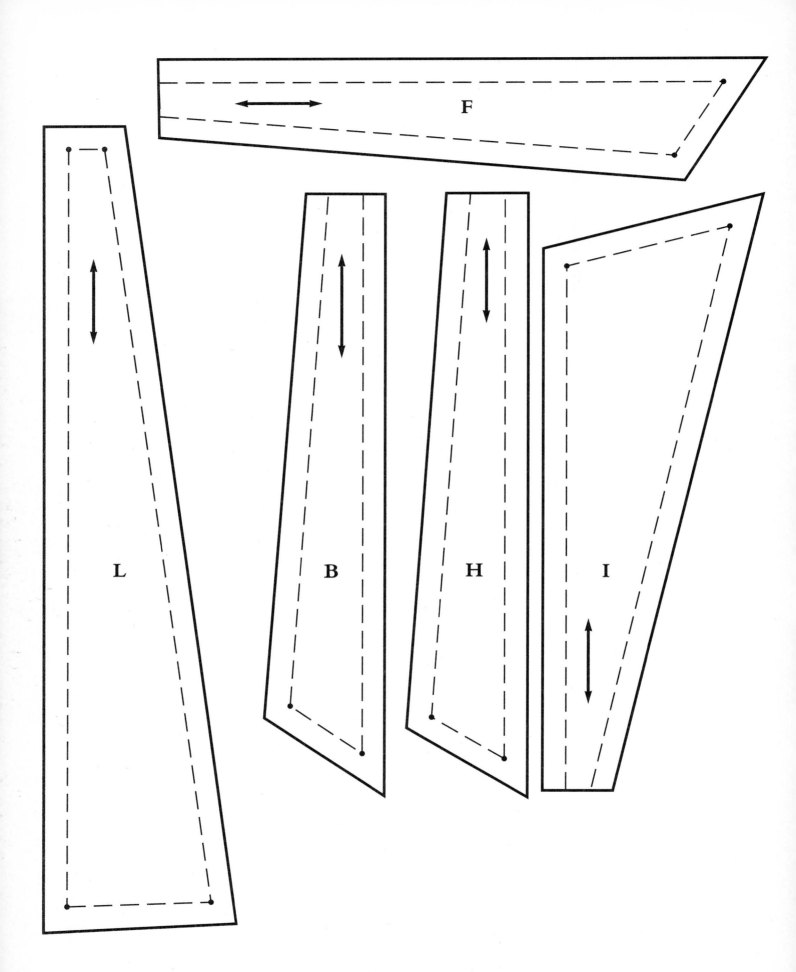

As an occupational therapist and a quilter, Cheryl takes a special interest in educating quilters on ways to avoid injuries while quilting. Such injuries as carpal tunnel syndrome and back and neck strain are common among stitchers, but avoidable, according to Cheryl. (See Cheryl's Guidelines for Preventing Repetitive Motion Injury for Quilters on the following page.)

"Over the years I've met many remarkable quilters who quilt despite their physical handicaps," says Cheryl. "I hope that by following their example and heeding my own advice, I can quilt forever. I can't imagine what life would be like without quilting!"

Cheryl Kagen

Cheektowaga, New York

Fans Charming
1990

Cheryl was inspired to make *Fans Charming* after studying a Victorian quilt entitled *Three-Dimensional Fans*. (See "Resources" for the source.) Both designs set the Friendship Fan block in a variation of the tumbling block arrangement. Cheryl's layout uniformly offsets each fan and its base with black to organize them into precise horizontal and vertical rows.

This quilt also displays Cheryl's collection of light and dark scraps from 541 different fabrics. When Cheryl moved to New York from the Midwest, the only part of her quilting accoutrements that went with her was her collection of five-inch squares of fabric. "I had every intention of making a charm quilt," she says, "but I became intrigued with this pattern. It contained three qualities of quilting that I especially enjoy: dimensionality, small pieces, and curves."

Fans Charming

Finished Quilt Size
44¼" x 49½"

Number of Blocks
54 Fan blocks

Fabric Requirements

Black	—1⅝ yd.
Dk. prints	—1½ yd. total
Lt. prints	—1½ yd. total
Black print for bias binding	—1 yd.
Backing	—1¾ yd.★

★60"-wide fabric

Number to Cut

Template A	—54 black★★
Template B	—54 lt. prints
Template C	—54 dk. prints
Template D	—54 lt. prints
Template E	—54 dk. prints
Template F	—54 lt. prints
Template G	—54 dk. prints
Template H	—54 lt. prints
Template I	—54 dk. prints
Template J	—54 lt. prints
	54 dk. prints
Template K	—40 black★★
Template L	—26 black★★
Template M	—4 black★★

★★See step 4 before cutting fabric.

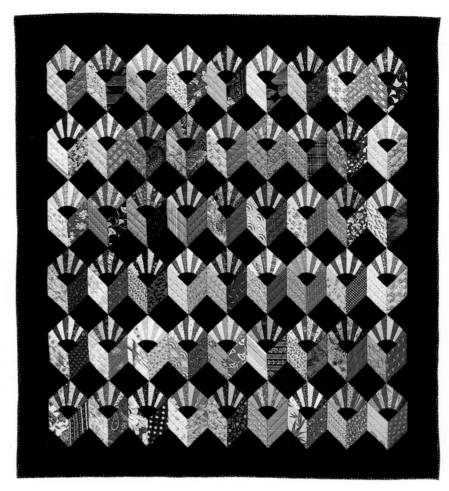

Quilt Top Assembly

1. Join fan blades (B through I), as shown in Block Piecing Diagram I. (Cheryl used different prints for each piece in a block, but all pieces were in the same color family. See quilt photograph.)

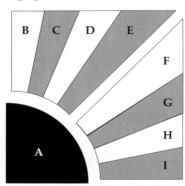

Block Piecing Diagram I

Join piece A to bottom of fan blades to make a square, as shown. Make 54.

Join a lt. and dk. print piece J to bottom of each fan square, as shown in Block Piecing Diagram II.

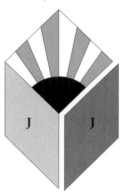

Block Piecing Diagram II

2. Arrange Fan blocks in 6 rows of 9 blocks each. Refer to quilt photograph for color arrangement. Join blocks at sides, as shown in Setting Diagram.
3. Alternate rows with squares (K) and end triangles (L), as shown in Setting Diagram. Carefully set-in squares (K) to bottoms of Fan blocks, except last row. Join triangles (L) to end of each row.

Join rows. Join triangles (L) to top and bottom of quilt. Join corner triangles (M).
4. Cut 2 borders, 3½"-wide, from black. Join to top and bottom of quilt. Cut 2 borders, 3½"-wide, from black. Join to sides of quilt.

Quilting

Quilt Fan blocks, as shown in Quilting Diagram and photograph. Background-quilt triangles (L) and border in ¼" double-line pattern, spaced 1¼" apart, on the diagonal.

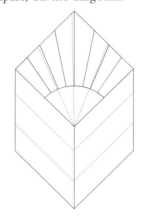

Quilting Diagram

Finished Edges
Bind with black print.

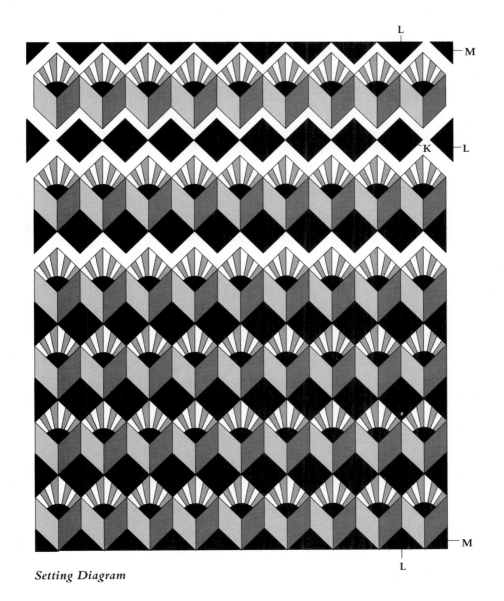

Setting Diagram

Guidelines for Prevention of Repetitive Motion Injury for Quilters

1. Use good posture when seated: hips and knees at right angles, lower back supported (with pillow if necessary). Make sure lighting is free of shadow and glare.

2. Make every effort to keep neck and wrists straight. This will most likely require propping both your arms and your work on small pillows.

3. Take frequent breaks: When you have been intensively using small muscles, get up at least once an hour to use large muscles—every 20 to 30 minutes is even better!

4. If you experience tingling, numbness, or recurring pain, see your doctor.

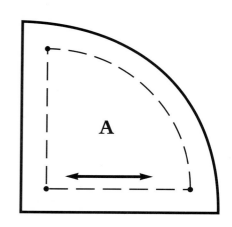

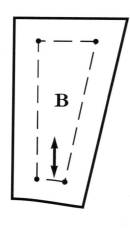

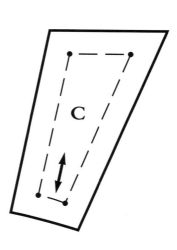

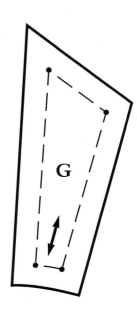

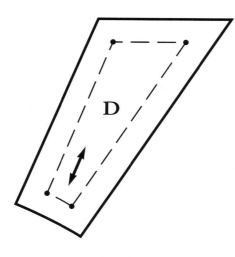

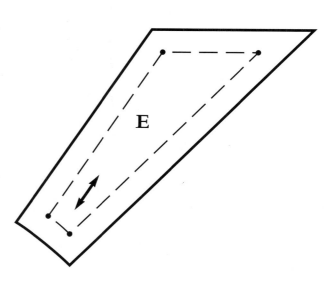

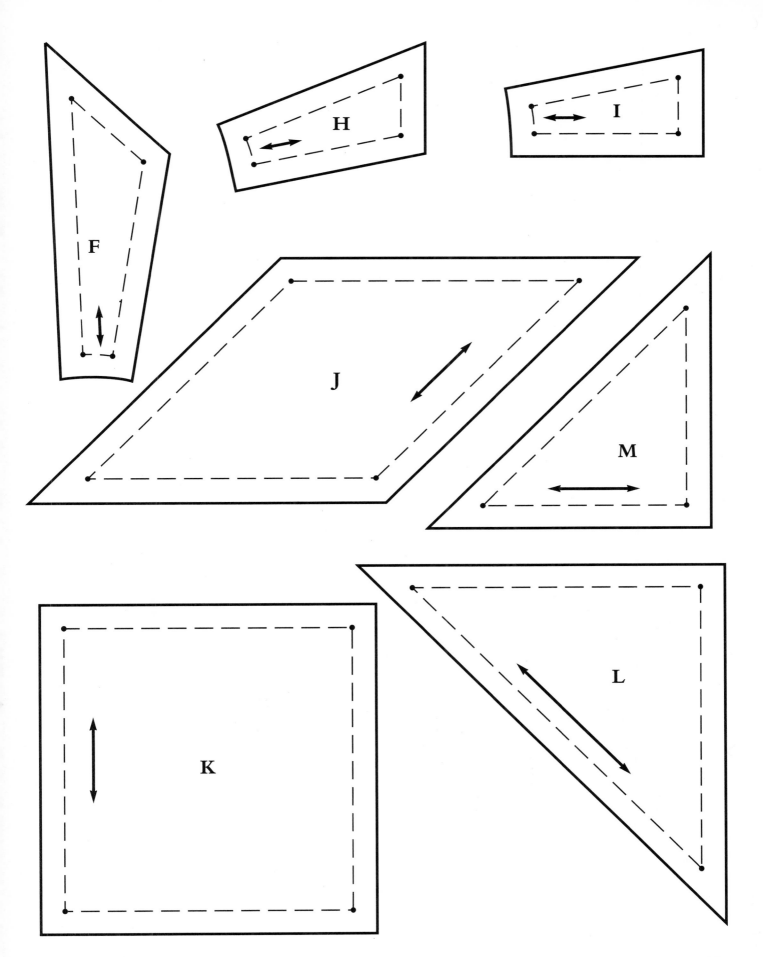

Scarlett Rose

Anderson, California

Scarlett is one of many quilters who became interested in quilt-making during America's Bicentennial. "Though I had been sewing since I was 12 years old," she says, "at the time of the Bicentennial, the historic craft of quiltmaking seemed the perfect medium in which to express myself creatively."

Attending quilt shows is one of Scarlett's favorite pastimes. "I can talk of nothing but quilts all day," she says, "with people I don't even know!" Scarlett is a member of the Quilter's Sew-ciety of Redding, California, and finds sharing her quilting experiences with friends most rewarding. "I have become aware that learning new quiltmaking techniques is a never-ending process," she says.

(A splash of autumn colors filled Scarlett's fabric palette when she made *Autumn Leaves*. You'll find her quilt with instructions in "Quilts Across America.")

Stars and Their Fans
1989

Scarlett calls this her "celebrity quilt" because while it was on display at a local quilt show, Richard Crenna was photographed admiring it. (See photograph.) In addition, the quilt stars in classes by well-known quilt teacher, Judy Mathieson, who uses slides of this quilt to demonstrate how Judy's Fan-cy Free Fan pattern (see "Resources") can be integrated into a nontraditional format.

The impetus for this quilt was an urge to do something with 60 star blocks Scarlett had made in 1983, using Jeffrey Gutcheon's method for elongating patterns. (See "Resources.") Six years later while participating in a workshop on fan blocks, Scarlett found a home for her star blocks. Fan blocks were made by members of the workshop, signed, and traded among themselves. Scarlett designed a setting for her stars and fans, assembled the quilt, and finished it with machine quilting.

Stars and Their Fans

Finished Quilt Size
94" x 102"

Fabric Requirements
Lt. prints★	—1 yd. total
Med./dk. prints★	—1 yd. total
Solids★	—1 yd. total
Misc. prints★★	—9 yd. total
Navy print	—3¼ yd.
Yellow	—2¾ yd.
Aqua	—1 yd.
Blue	—1 yd.
Pink	—1 yd.
Rose	—1 yd.
Lavender	—1 yd.
Navy print for bias binding	—1¼ yd.
Backing	—8¾ yd.

★For Fans
★★For Texas Stars and setting pieces

Number to Cut
Template A	—18 lt. prints‡
Template B	—18 med./dk. prints‡
Template C	—18 lt. prints‡
Template D	—18 med./dk. prints‡
Template E	—18 lt. prints‡
Template F	—18 med./dk. prints‡
Template G	—18 lt. prints‡
Template H	—18 med./dk. prints‡
Template I	—18 lt. prints‡
Template J	—18 med./dk. prints‡
Template K	—18 solids‡
Template L	—18 solids‡
Template M	—12 aqua
	12 blue
	12 pink
Template M#	—12 aqua
	12 blue
	12 pink
Template N	—100 misc. prints##
Template O	—320 misc. prints##
Template P	—6 rose
	6 lavender
Template Q	—8 misc. prints
8½" square	—18 misc. prints

‡For each Fan, cut A, C, E, G, and I from 1 lt. print; cut B, D, F, H, and J from 1 med./dk. print; and cut K and L from 1 solid.
#Flip or turn over template if fabric is one-sided.
##For each Texas Star, cut 4 pieces (N) and 8 pieces (O) from 1 print, and cut 1 piece (N) and 8 pieces (O) from another print. Flip or turn over Template (O) for half of the pieces if fabric is one-sided. See Texas Star Piecing Diagram.

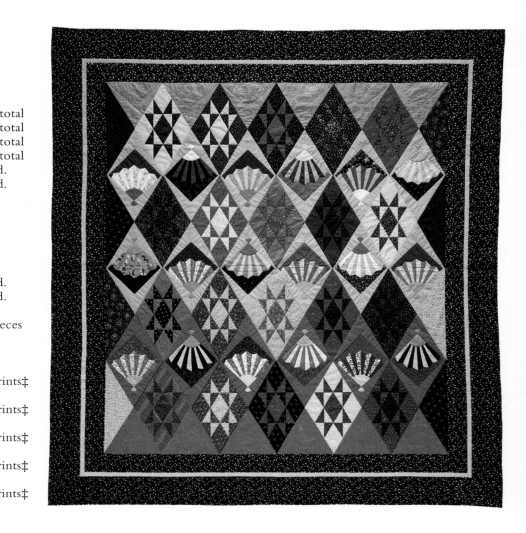

Quilt Top Assembly
1. Coordinate fabric colors of fan pieces (A through L) to make 18 fans. Join fan blades (A through J) at sides, as shown in Fan Piecing Diagram I.

Appliqué fans to squares. Trim fabric from behind each fan, leaving ¼" seam allowance.

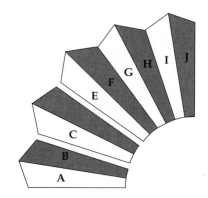

Fan Piecing Diagram I

Appliqué pieces (K) to fan blades. Coordinate fabric colors and place each fan in corner of 8½" square, as shown in Fan Piecing Diagram II.

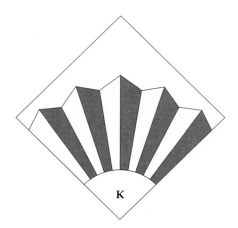

Fan Piecing Diagram II

Join 4 pieces (M) of 1 color to each fan square, as shown in Fan Diamond Piecing Diagram. Appliqué piece (L) to each fan, as shown.

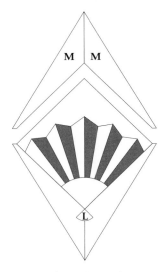

Fan Diamond Piecing Diagram

2. Coordinate fabric colors of Texas Star pieces (N and O) to make 20 Texas Star diamonds.

Join 4 triangles (O) to form a pieced diamond, as shown in Texas Star Piecing Diagram. Make 4 pieced diamonds. Join pieced diamonds with diamonds (N) to form 3 rows, as shown. Join rows to complete diamond.

Texas Star Piecing Diagram

3. Alternate Fan diamonds with Texas Star diamonds to form diagonal rows, as shown in Setting Diagram. Join diamonds at sides and join setting triangles (P and Q) to ends of rows, as

Setting Diagram

shown. (Lavender setting triangles (P) are at the top and rose at the bottom.) Join rows.

4. Cut 4 borders, 4½" wide, from navy print. Join to quilt and miter corners.

Cut 4 borders, 1½" wide, from yellow. Join to quilt and miter corners.

Cut 4 borders, 6½" wide, from navy print. Join to quilt and miter corners.

Machine Quilting
Quilt in-the-ditch of all diagonal seams. Outline-quilt outside seam lines of fans, stars, inner quilt, and yellow border. Using template M, mark quilting lines to form a triangle in each setting triangle P and stitch. Stitch parallel lines, 2" apart, along length of navy print borders.

Finished Edges
Bind with navy print.

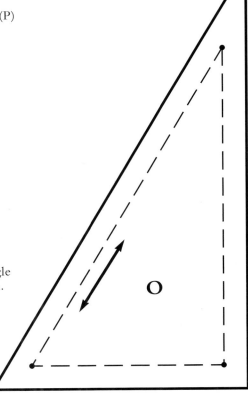

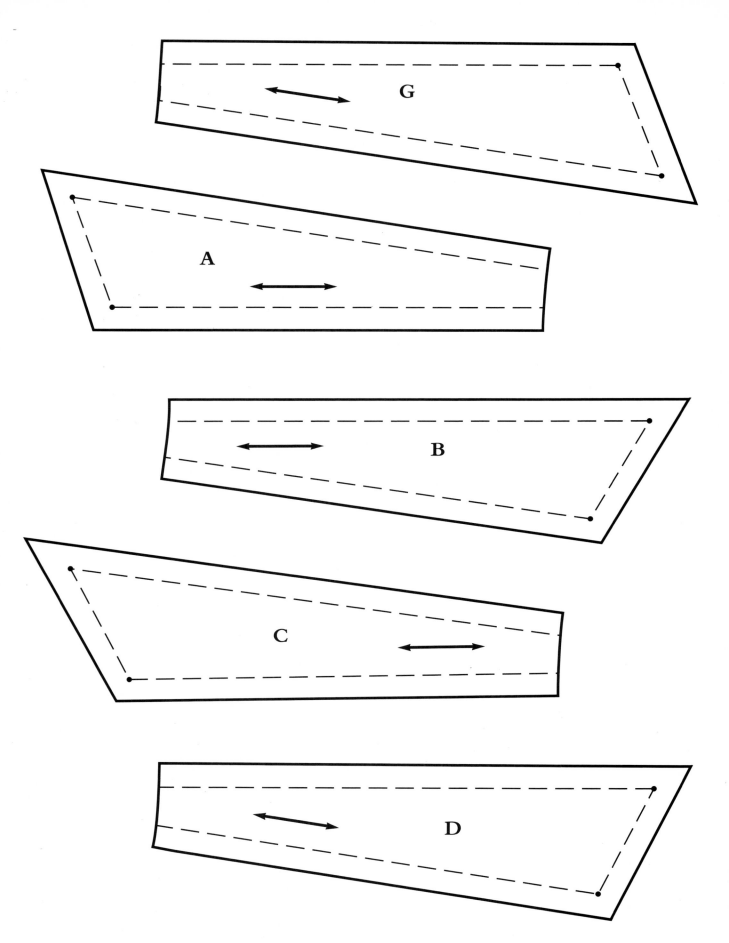

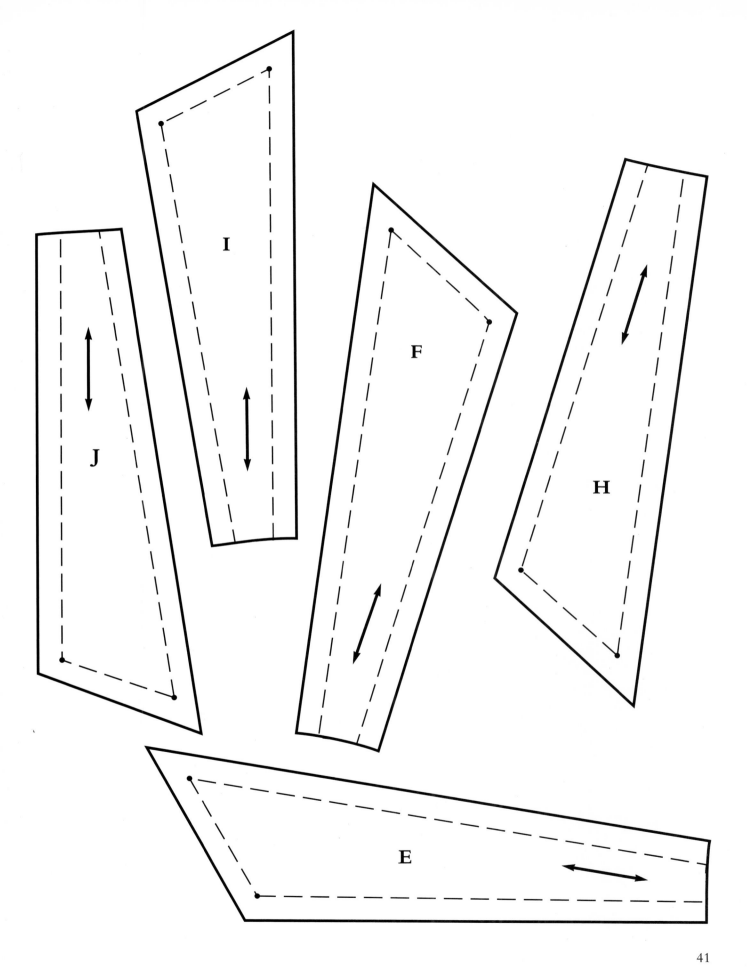

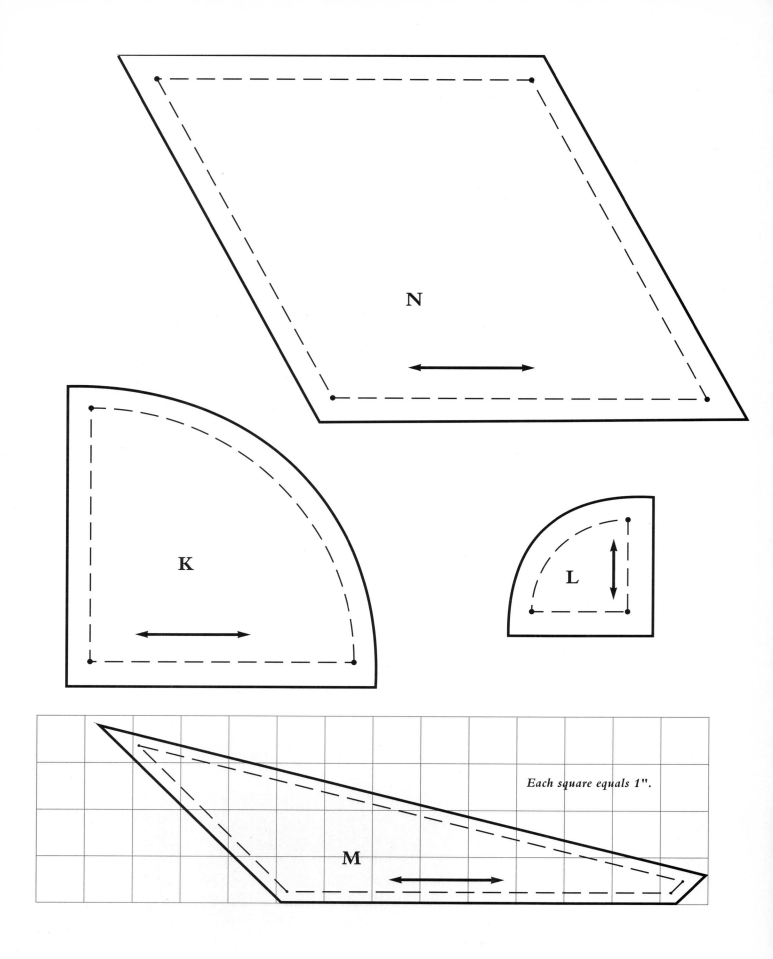

N

K

L

M

Each square equals 1".

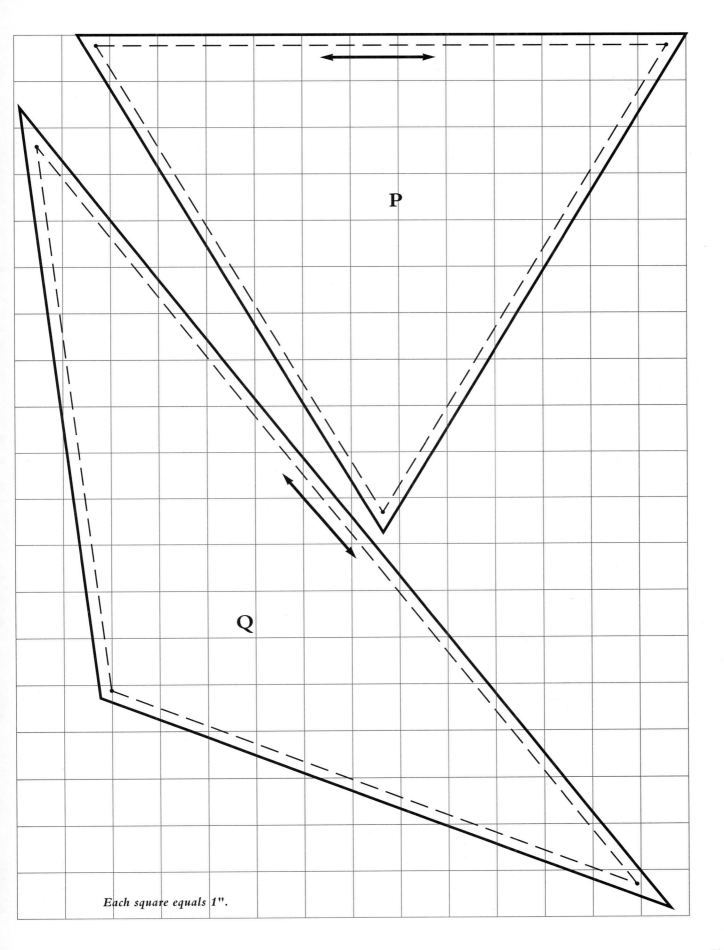

P

Q

Each square equals 1".

Janice Eggleston

Corinth, New York

Because Janice finds every step of quilting a pleasure, she works on several projects at various stages simultaneously. "Also, for variety's sake," says Janice, "I'll often make an appliquéd quilt after completing a patchwork one."

Janice is a member of two guilds, the Wings Falls Quilter's Guild and the Hudson River Piecemaker's Quilt Guild. She credits them with introducing her to advanced quilting techniques and especially enjoys the quilt competitions. "I must confess," she says, "I have been thoroughly bitten by the quilting bug!"

Fan-T-See
1989

The Eccentric Star block takes on a new personality with Janice's eye-catching color placement. Two tones of one color, paired in triangular sets, become the blades for the whirling fans.

Planning a quilt is Janice's favorite part of quiltmaking, and numerous colored-pencil sketches were made before developing the right formula for *Fan-T-See*. The scalloped border edging complements the curvature of the vine of opened fans.

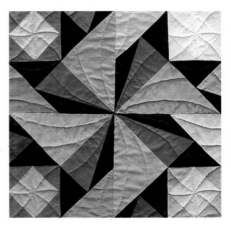

Fan–T–See

Finished Quilt Size
73" x 82"

Number of Blocks and Finished Size
42 blocks—9" x 9"

Fabric Requirements

Lavender	—¾ yd.
Purple	—⅝ yd.
Aqua	—¾ yd.
Dk. aqua	—⅝ yd.
Yellow	—⅝ yd.
Dk. yellow	—⅝ yd.
Lt. red	—¾ yd.
Red	—¾ yd.
Green	—⅜ yd.
Dk. green	—⅜ yd.
Lt. green	—¾ yd.
Med. green	—1⅝ yd.★
Blue	—⅝ yd.
Dk. blue	—½ yd.
Rose	—⅝ yd.
Dk. rose	—½ yd.
Lt. orange	—⅝ yd.
Dk. orange	—⅝ yd.
Gray	—1⅛ yd.
Med. gray	—1 yd.
Black	—4 yd.
Black for bias binding	—1½ yd.
Backing	—5 yd.

★Includes 1 yd. for continuous bias strip for vine.

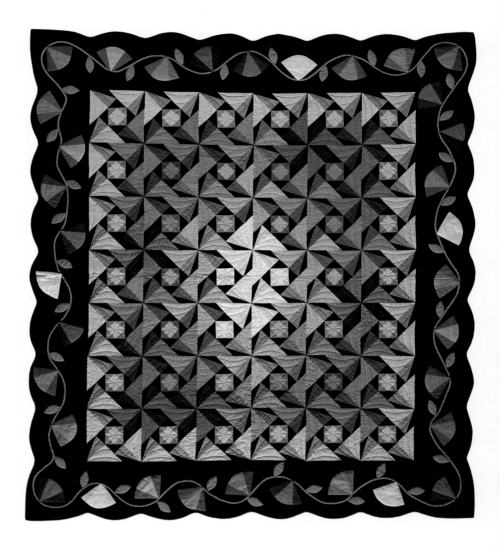

Number to Cut

Template A	—2 lavender
	2 aqua
	2 yellow
	1 dk. yellow
	4 lt. red
	4 lt. green
	5 lt. orange
	22 gray
Template B	—8 purple
	8 dk. aqua
	4 yellow
	8 dk. yellow
	16 red
	16 med. green
	20 dk. orange
	88 med. gray
Template C	—168 black
Template D	—24 lavender
	16 aqua
	8 yellow
	(continued)

Template D	—16 lt. red
	8 green
	12 lt. green
	12 blue
	12 rose
	12 lt. orange
	48 gray
Template E	—24 purple
	16 dk. aqua
	8 dk. yellow
	16 red
	8 dk. green
	12 med. green
	12 dk. blue
	12 dk. rose
	12 dk. orange
	48 med. gray
Template F	—168 black
Template G	—4 lavender
	6 aqua
	5 yellow
	(continued)

Template G	—6 lt. red
	4 blue
	5 rose
	4 lt. orange
Template H	—4 purple
	6 dk. aqua
	5 dk. yellow
	6 red
	4 dk. blue
	5 dk. rose
	4 dk. orange
Template H★★	—4 purple
	6 dk. aqua
	5 dk. yellow
	6 red
	4 dk. blue
	5 dk. rose
	4 dk. orange
Template I	—36 med. green★★★

★★Flip or turn over template if fabric is one-sided.

★★★See step 5 before cutting fabric.

Quilt Top Assembly

1. As you cut pieces, arrange them in blocks and rows, as shown in Setting Diagram. Group pieces for each block and pin together. Stack blocks in order for each row and label with row number.

2. Join block center section and side sections, as shown in Block Piecing Diagram I.

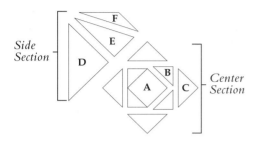

Block Piecing Diagram I

Join side sections to center section using partial seaming technique. Refer to Block Piecing Diagram II and join first side section (1) to center section, stopping at point marked X.

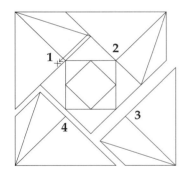

Block Piecing Diagram II

Join remaining side sections in clockwise order, as shown. Complete seam of side section 1. Make 42 blocks.

3. Arrange 6 blocks in 7 rows, as shown in Setting Diagram, and check block placement. Join blocks at sides to form rows and join rows.

4. Cut 2 borders, 10" wide, from black for sides of quilt. Join to quilt. Cut 2 borders, 10" wide, from black for top and bottom of quilt. Join to quilt.

5. Make continuous bias strip, ¾" wide, from med. green for border vine. Pin bias strip to border, as shown in photograph, and appliqué.

6. Put 2 fan pieces (H) of one color with fan piece (G) of same color family. Join fan pieces (H) to opposite

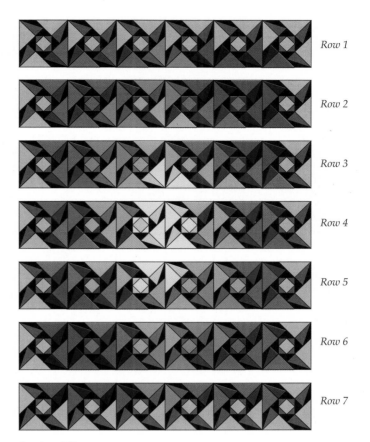

Setting Diagram

sides of fan piece (G) to complete fan. Repeat for each color family and make 34 fans.

Arrange fans and leaves (I) on vine and appliqué in place.

7. Make a template from guideline for scalloped edge. The expanse of the curve is 9"; therefore, intersections of curves will correspond with block-to-block seam lines.

Begin marking border outward from center seam of inner quilt for top and bottom borders and at row 4 seam for sides. Stop marking scallops at border seam lines.

For corners, mark curve on its upward side only but instead of marking downward curve, draw a straight line from curve's midpoint to quilt edge to make a flared and pointed corner. (See quilt photograph and Diagram on pattern page.)

Leave scalloped edges uncut until quilting is complete.

Quilting

Quilt inner quilt with curved lines, as shown in Quilting Diagram.

Outline-quilt outside seam lines of appliquéd pieces. Background-quilt border with a 3" cross-hatching grid.

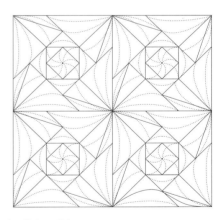

Quilting Diagram

Finished Edges

With right sides facing, sew a continuous bias strip of black for binding to quilt top along marked lines for scallops. Ease bias strip on outside curves and pivot at point on inside curves. Trim all layers to ¼" seam allowance. Miter or tuck inside curves. Turn binding to back and blindstitch in place.

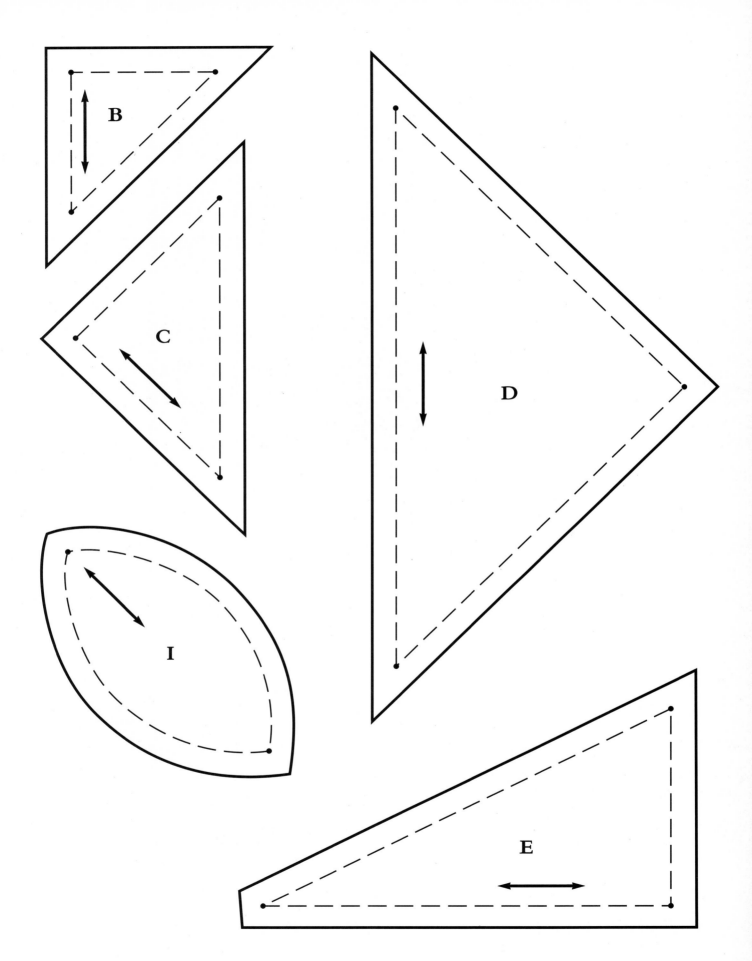

B

C

D

I

E

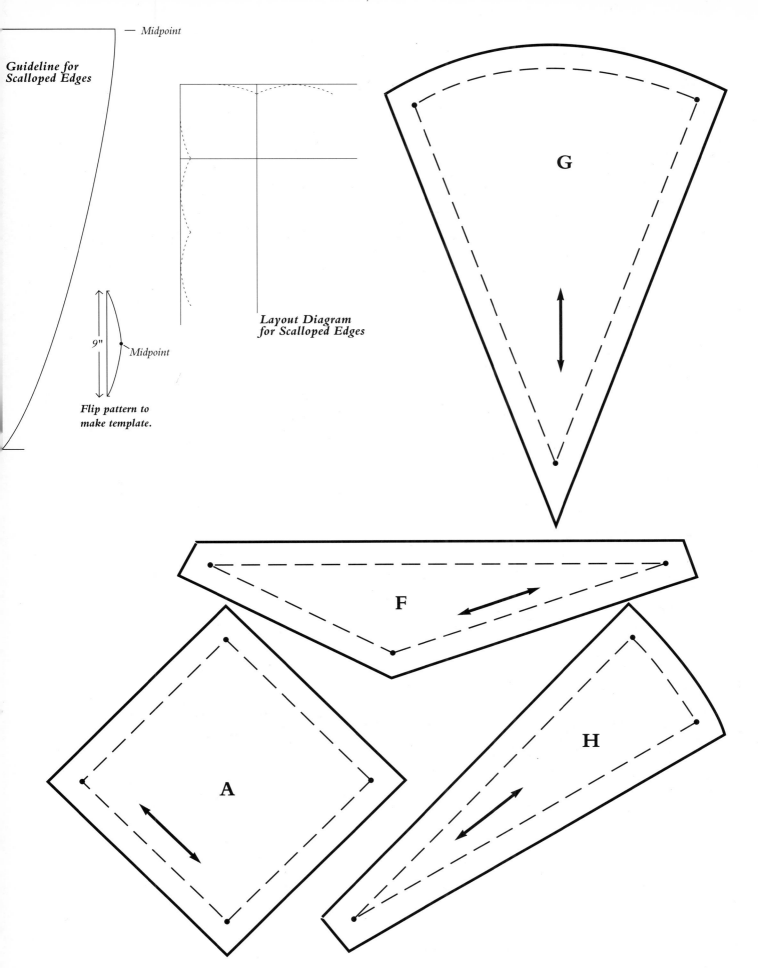

Midpoint

Guideline for Scalloped Edges

9"

Midpoint

Flip pattern to make template.

Layout Diagram for Scalloped Edges

G

F

A

H

QUILTS
ACROSS
AMERICA

Scarlett Rose

Anderson, California

After you get to know Scarlett, you're not surprised to learn that she works in a fabric store. "I can't imagine not having any fabric around or not sewing," says Scarlett. "The satisfaction that I get from working with fabrics and making quilts is wonderful."

While teaching quiltmaking, Scarlett makes a point of sharing her good experiences as well as her not-so-good ones. "I believe their knowing that I made some of the same mistakes that they make puts my students at ease," says Scarlett.

Take time to enjoy another one of Scarlett's successful quilts in "Fabulous Fans."

Autumn Leaves
1983

This interlocking leaf pattern has been popular with quilters since it was first introduced in a Nancy Page column in the 1920s. Scarlett's *Autumn Leaves* rounds up all the colors of autumn and pours them into one setting. The setting is barn-raising, which Scarlett borrowed from Log Cabin quilts. To make sure that the leaves are set correctly, she recommends that quilters carefully lay out their rows before assembling them. In addition, Scarlett appliquéd triangles in the borders to make every leaf complete. Each leaf is hand-quilted with a large leaf pattern.

Autumn Leaves

Finished Quilt Size
95" x 95"

Number of Blocks and Finished Size
81 blocks—9" x 9"

Fabric Requirements

Green prints — 1⅞ yd. total
Orange prints — 1⅞ yd. total
Brown prints — 1⅞ yd. total
Yellow prints — 1⅞ yd. total
Red prints — 1⅞ yd. total
Black prints★ — 5¼ yd. total
Backing — 8¼ yd.
★Select 2⅞ yd. of 1 fabric for border. See step 3.

Number to Cut

Template A — 16 green prints
16 orange prints
16 brown prints
17 yellow prints
16 red prints
Template B — 64 green prints
64 orange prints
64 brown prints
68 yellow prints
64 red prints
18 black prints
Template C — 16 green prints
16 orange prints
16 brown prints
17 yellow prints
16 red prints
Template D — 156 black prints

Quilt Top Assembly

1. Arrange all pieces for inner quilt in rows, as shown in Block Piecing Diagram and Setting Diagram I. (This is necessary to ensure proper color arrangement.) You will have 18 triangle Bs left over; these will be appliquéd to border in step 3.

Pick up pieces in blocks and pin them together until ready for assembly. Stack pinned blocks in order for each row and label rows. "It is important to keep them in order," says Scarlett, "since parts of each leaf (triangle Bs) extend into neighboring blocks."

2. Join block pieces, as shown in Block Piecing Diagram. Join blocks to form rows and join rows. (See Setting Diagrams I and II.)

3. Cut 4 borders, 7½" wide, from 1 black print. Place each border right side up alongside quilt edge. (Border corners will be mitered.) Align

remaining triangles (B) with blocks, matching fabrics as shown in Setting Diagram II and quilt photograph. With 1 raw edge of triangle aligned with raw edge of border, appliqué triangles to border. Join borders to quilt and miter corners.

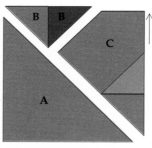

Block Piecing Diagram

Quilting
Quilt leaf pattern in center of each block.

Finished Edges
Fold each square (D), as shown in Prairie Point Folding Diagrams. Arrange 39 prairie points in a continuous, overlapping fashion along each side of quilt, as shown in Prairie Point Arrangement Diagram. Baste prairie points together.

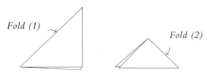

Fold (1)   *Fold (2)*

Prairie Point Folding Diagrams

Prairie Point Arrangement Diagram

With right sides facing and raw edges aligned, stitch prairie points to quilt top, as shown in Prairie Point Attachment Diagrams. Turn under raw edge of quilt backing to cover raw edges of prairie points and blindstitch in place.

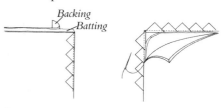

Backing
Batting

I

Prairie Point Attachment Diagrams

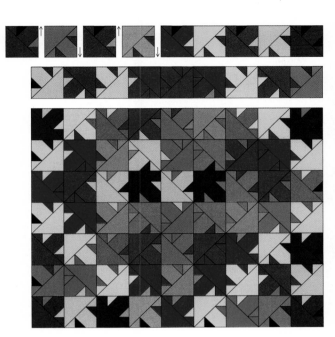

Setting Diagram I

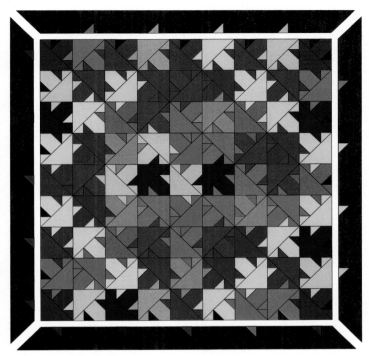

Setting Diagram II

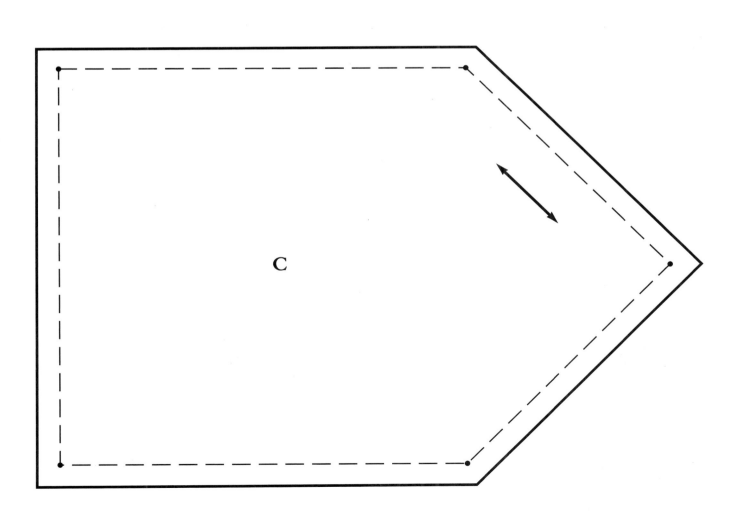

C

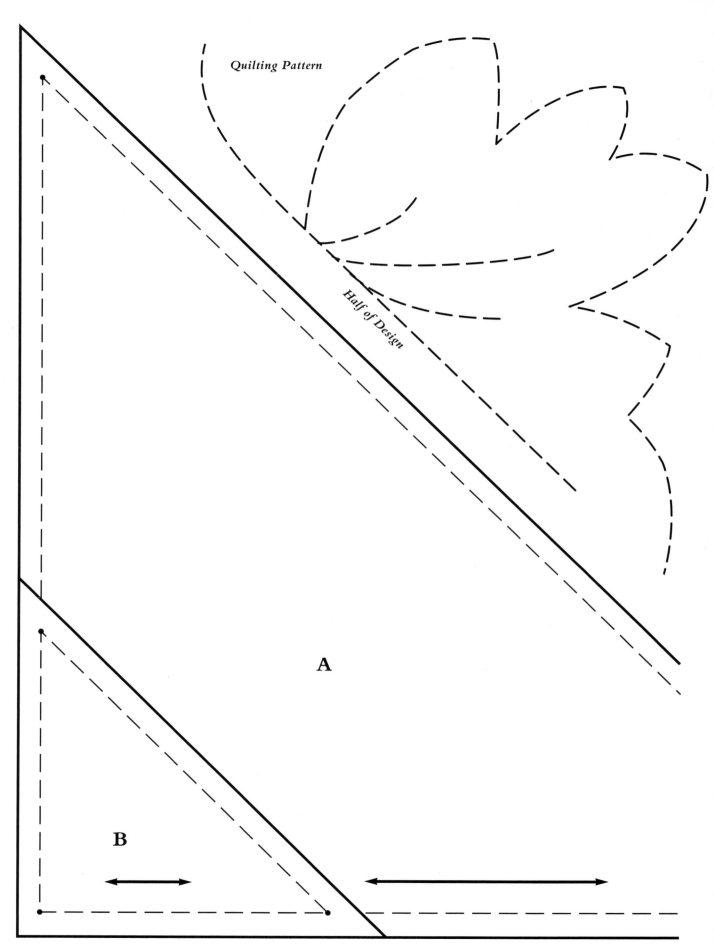

Quilting Pattern

Half of Design

A

B

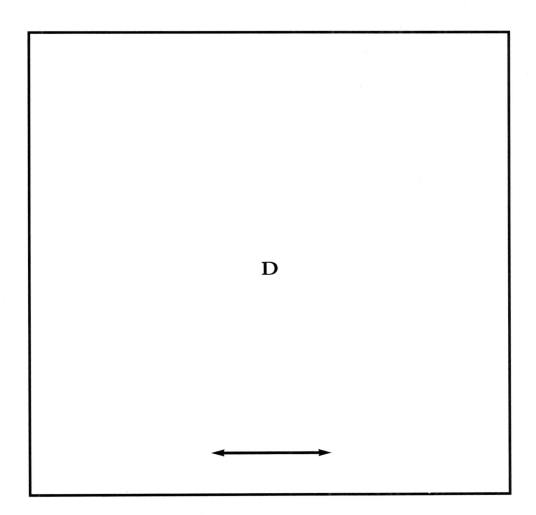

D

Shaded portion indicates overlap from preceding page.

Maria V. Cobb

Anchorage, Alaska

Quilting for Maria, as for many others, has filled what might have been empty hours during those first months of retirement. "I was very bored at home all day," says Maria, "so I enrolled in a quilt-making class. Boy, am I ever glad I did!"

Maria is often up at 5:00 a.m. to quilt—an example of her devotion to this craft. "My quilts do not need to win ribbons nor to be exhibited," says Maria. "I just want them to be pleasing to look at and to touch."

Ties and Diamonds
1989

Maria took her stored pink and black fabrics and set about designing a quilt that had a feeling of constant movement. "I am a very active person now," says Maria, "but I wanted to have a quilt on the wall that, as I got older, would get me up and moving!"

Single and double bow tie blocks are alternated and rotated to obtain this dazzling geometric design. The color inspiration came from Maria's teenage years when Elvis influenced the retail industry with his favorite colors of pink and black.

Ties and Diamonds

Finished Quilt Size
48" x 48"

Number of Blocks and Finished Size
36 blocks—8" x 8"

Fabric Requirements

Hot pink I	—½ yd.
Hot pink II	—⅝ yd.
Fuchsia	—⅜ yd.
Pink print I	—¾ yd.
Pink print II	—⅝ yd.
Pink floral	—½ yd.
Purple	—⅜ yd.
Gray floral	—¾ yd.
Lt. gray print	—½ yd.
Black print I	—½ yd.
Black print II	—½ yd.
Black print III	—½ yd.
Black print IV	—⅜ yd.
Black print V	—⅜ yd.
Black for bias binding	—1 yd.
Backing	—3 yd.

Other Materials
Pink quilting thread

Number to Cut

Template A —8 hot pink I
8 hot pink II
8 pink print I
24 gray floral
8 black print I

Template B —8 hot pink I
4 hot pink II
4 pink print I
8 pink print II
16 pink floral

Template C —8 hot pink I
4 hot pink II
8 fuchsia
4 pink print I
8 pink print II
40 lt. gray print

Template D —16 hot pink I
8 hot pink II
8 pink print I
8 pink print II
8 pink floral
32 black print II
32 black print III
16 black print IV
8 black print V

Template E —16 hot pink I
8 hot pink II
8 fuchsia
8 pink print I
32 pink print II
32 pink floral
4 lt. gray print
(continued)

Template E —32 black print II
32 black print III
16 black print IV
8 black print V

Template F —8 pink floral
24 gray floral
8 black print I

Template G —16 hot pink I
16 hot pink II
12 fuchsia
16 pink print I
16 pink print II

Template H —16 hot pink II
8 pink print II
24 lt. gray print

Template I —8 pink print I

Template J —8 pink print II

Template K —4 pink print II

Template K★ —4 pink print II

★Flip or turn over template if fabric is one-sided.

Quilt Top Assembly
1. Follow piecing diagrams for blocks 1A through 7 and piece number of blocks indicated. Arrange fabric colors, as shown, before piecing blocks. (Arrows indicate tops of blocks.)
2. Arrange blocks in sections, as shown in Setting Diagram I. Join sections, as shown in Setting Diagram II.

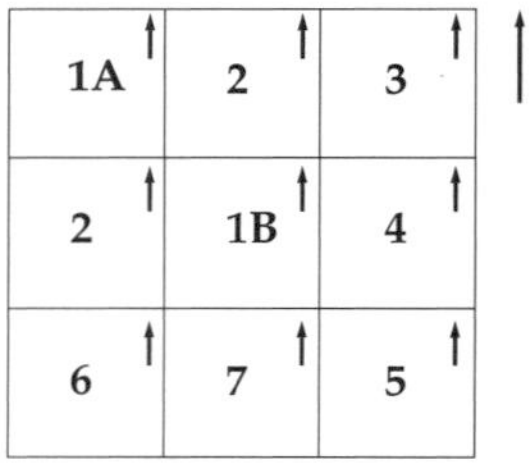

1A ↑	2 ↑	3 ↑	↑
2 ↑	1B ↑	4 ↑	
6 ↑	7 ↑	5 ↑	

Section I—Make 2.

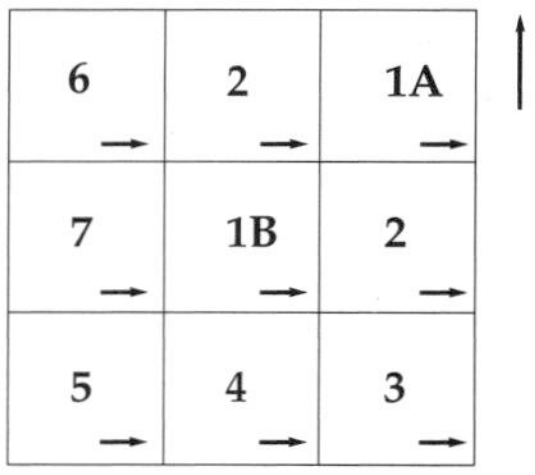

6	2	1A	↑
→	→	→	
7	1B	2	
→	→	→	
5	4	3	
→	→	→	

Section II—Make 2.

Setting Diagram I

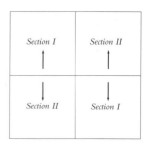

Section I ↑	Section II ↑
Section II ↓	Section I ↓

Setting Diagram II

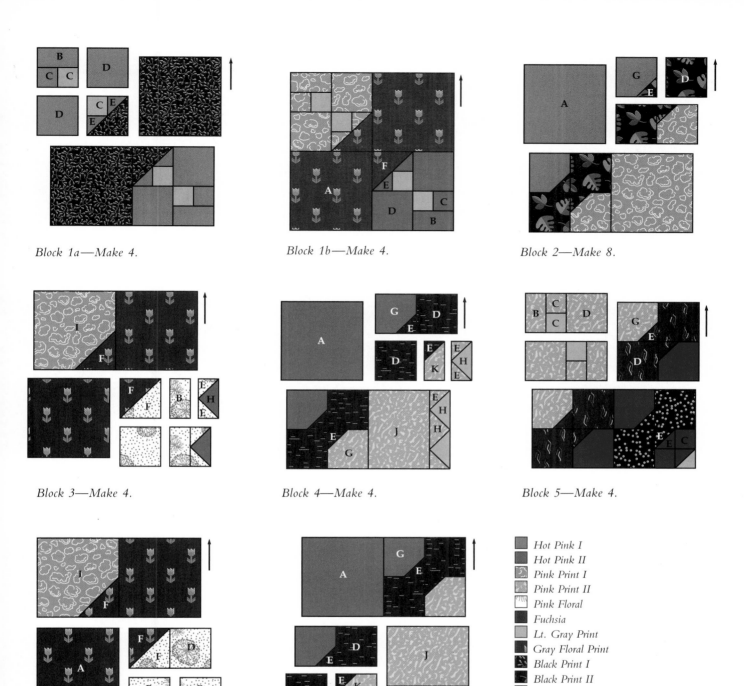

Block 1a—Make 4.

Block 1b—Make 4.

Block 2—Make 8.

Block 3—Make 4.

Block 4—Make 4.

Block 5—Make 4.

Block 6—Make 4.

Block 7—Make 4.

Hot Pink I
Hot Pink II
Pink Print I
Pink Print II
Pink Floral
Fuchsia
Lt. Gray Print
Gray Floral Print
Black Print I
Black Print II
Black Print III
Black Print IV
Black Print V

Block Piecing Diagrams

Quilting

Outline-quilt bow tie pieces ¼" inside seam lines. Quilt remaining areas in diagonal lines, 1" apart. (See quilt photograph.)

Finished Edges

For flange along binding, cut 4 strips, 1"-wide, from purple. With wrong sides facing, fold strips in half lengthwise. With raw edges aligned, join to quilt and miter corners.

Bind with black fabric.

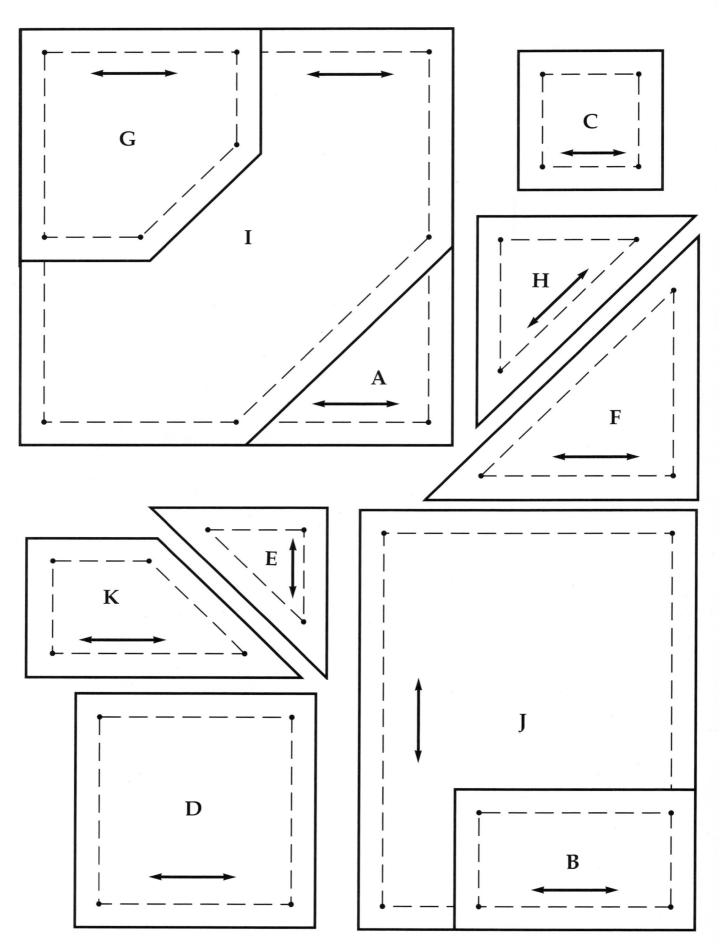

Katy J. Widger

Los Lunas, New Mexico

Katy learned to quilt after years of sewing, crocheting, stained-glass projects, and many other crafts. "When I started quiltmaking," says Katy, "I didn't have the slightest idea what I was getting into—either in the construction or the pleasure—that I was opening the door to all the future quilts I would make. You see, making quilts has been for me like eating tortilla chips—you can't make just one!"

One other thing about quiltmaking that Katy likes to share is that it has provided a wonderful healing therapy. "When I learned that it would be nearly impossible for me to bear children," says Katy, "I also learned to let go of my intense desire to be a mother and to channel the creativity within me into making quilts. The color, warmth, and softness of my quilts have helped to heal a great wound inside me."

Turn to "Designer Gallery" to view Katy's fabric interpretation of a New Mexico summer sunset.

Leah's Quilt: Child's Play
1990

Is there a budding young artist in your life whose drawings are too special to throw away? The drawings hang on the refrigerator door for a few weeks, and if fingerprints and ketchup don't do them in, they are destined for the hall closet, rarely to be seen again. Katy felt that her stepdaughter Leah's artistic talent deserved to be recognized and thought what better way than in a quilt. When Leah was eight years old, Katy asked her to draw eight different drawings, using heat transfer crayons.

Katy dyed and handprinted the fabrics used for the framing strips and border. Hand-printing was done using stamps, carved from potatoes, sponges, leaves, and a variety of other items. (Our instructions give fabric requirements for purchased printed fabric. If you are interested in painting and stamping your own fabrics, see "Resources.")

Katy made a traditional House block and set it in the center with Leah's drawings surrounding it. Choose your favorite block for the center or use nine drawings, as instructed below, instead of eight. Katy used the method devised by Jeanne Benson (a featured quilter on page 25) for skewed Log Cabin framing strips.

Fabrics with heat-transfer crayon imprints can be washed in warm water and a mild detergent on gentle cycle. Do not use bleach or place the quilt in the dryer.

Leah's Quilt: Child's Play

Finished Quilt Size
53½" x 53½"

Number of Blocks and Finished Size
9 blocks—16" x 16"

Fabric Requirements
White★   —1½ yd.
Border print★★   —2½ yd.
Pink   —1½ yd.
8 prints★★★   —¼ yd. each
8 solids★★★   —¼ yd. each
Backing   —3¼ yd.

★Select a cotton/polyester blend and wash fabric before transferring drawings. See step 2.

★★Select a bright-colored print to match crayon colors. Yardage for bias binding is included.

★★★Prints and solids are used for framing strips. Select colors to match crayon colors.

Other Materials
Heat transfer crayons
  (Crayola no. 5008)
Machine embroidery threads,
  variegated and to match backing
  for machine quilting
Newspapers
White butcher paper

Quilt Top Assembly

1. Cut nine 13" squares from butcher paper. Center and draw a 12½" square on each butcher paper square. (The drawn square serves as a boundary for the drawings.)

Have the child draw pictures using crayons. The child should press very firmly with the crayons and cover the entire 12½" square.

2. Cut nine 13" squares from white fabric. Place a stack of newspapers on ironing board and top stack with a clean sheet of butcher paper. Lay white fabric square on top of paper stack.

Brush excess crayon specks from each drawing. Lay 1 drawing face down on top of fabric, matching edges. Place another clean sheet of butcher paper on top of drawing.

Using a dry iron set on "cotton," apply steady pressure over entire drawing until drawing becomes slightly visible through back of papers. Lift iron from place to place, because sliding it across surface may blur image.

Carefully separate drawing from fabric. (Drawing can be reused if more crayon is applied.) Repeat for each drawing. Trim each fabric square to 12½".

3. For framing strips, cut across prints and solids to make 2¼" wide strips. Using Log Cabin piecing technique

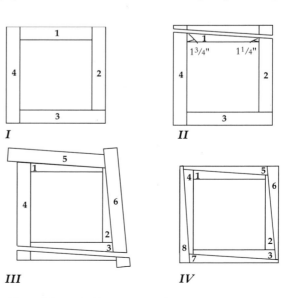

Skewed Log Cabin Frame Diagrams

and ¼" seams, join 1 round of strips to each square, as shown in Skewed Log Cabin Frame Diagram I. Alternate solid and print strips in a clockwise direction as shown. (See quilt photograph.) Stop after fourth strip is joined.

Measure and mark 1¾" from square seam line across framing strip 1 at left and 1¼" at right, as shown in Diagram II. Connect marks, drawing a line over framing strips at an angle. Trim along line. Join a print framing strip to new edge.

Repeat for remaining sides, as shown in Diagram III.

When round 2 strips have been joined, trim framing strips to make a 16½" block. (See Diagram IV.) Repeat for each square.

4. Arrange blocks in 3 rows of 3 blocks each. Join blocks at sides to form rows and join rows.

5. Cut border print and pink into 5" x 14" rectangles. Group rectangles in sets of 4: 2 border print and 2 pink. With raw edges aligned, stack rectangle sets and cut across fabrics at random angles to form wedges. Wedges should be cut wide enough to include seam allowances so that finished pieces do not come to a point. (See pieces after joining in Border Piecing Diagram I.)

Alternate 2 border print wedges with 2 pink wedges from 1 stack, as shown in Diagram I, and join to form units. (When joining wedges from the same stack, they will fit together and form rectangles. Therefore, little fabric is wasted.)

Cut across units to make 4 segments, as shown in Diagram II. (Again, cut segments wide enough to include seam allowances so that finished pieces do not come to a point.) Repeat until all wedges have been joined and segments cut.

Alternate segments in random manner and join to make 4 long strips for borders. Trim long edges even so that each strip is 3¼" wide. Join borders to opposite sides of quilt.

Join remaining borders to top and bottom of quilt.

Machine Quilting
Katy used variegated thread in top spool and a thread color to match backing in bobbin. Machine-quilt selected areas of each drawing. For example, Katy straightstitched the outline of the airplane, the pilot, and the cloud. (See block photograph.)

Use a ⅛"-wide and 12-stitch-length zigzag stitch to quilt over seams of block framing strips. (See block photograph.)

Finished Edges
Bind with border print.

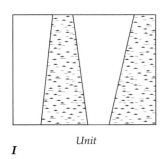

Unit

I

Border Piecing Diagram

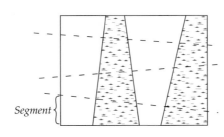

Segment

II

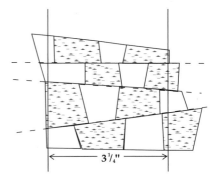

3¼"

III

Four Corners

1988

The Four Corners area of New Mexico is where the borders of New Mexico, Colorado, Utah, and Arizona meet. While living in the area, Katy was taken by the beauty of the landscape and influenced by the artistry of the Navajo Indians who lived there. "With this quilt," says Katy, "I am expressing the insistent yet subtle color changes that take place almost daily in the West, where earth and sky reflect the gradual shift from hue to hue in an everchanging palette."

To accurately present this palette, Katy dyed fabric in five steps between complementary colors blue and orange to get 18 different shades. Three-inch squares, arranged in a Navajo-style pattern, are "underquilted" by machine and intermittently accented with prairie points for a three-dimensional effect.

Four Corners

Finished Quilt Size
62½" x 80"

Fabric Requirements
Orange to blue (18 values)	— ½ yd. each
Blue for bias binding	— 1 yd.
Backing and facing	— 5½ yd.

Other Materials
Bicycle clips
Thread to match backing for machine quilting

Quilt Top Assembly
1. Cut across each fabric for quilt top to make 3"-wide strips. Cut strips into 3" squares.

2. Arrange squares in 25 vertical rows, as shown in Setting Diagram. (Note that row arrangement has an 8-row repeat.)

Make prairie points from light blue and attach to top of squares with ¼" seam. (See page 54, Finished Edges, for instructions for making prairie points.) Stack squares in rows and label rows.

3. Join squares to form rows. Iron seam allowances of odd-numbered

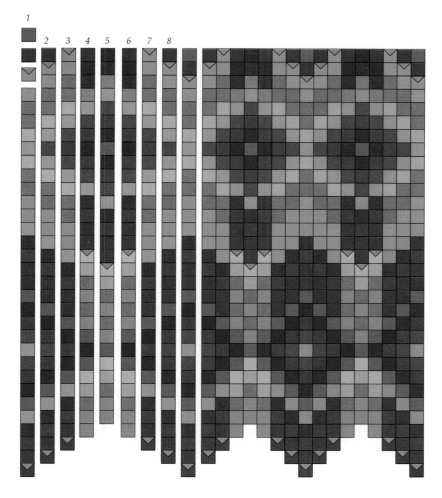

Setting Diagram

rows up and even-numbered rows down. Join rows.

Underquilting
After layering quilt, fold quilt top back from *right to left* to expose vertical seam allowance of row 1. Smooth quilt top and place straight pins at top of row 1 seam allowance and at seam allowance intersections of each square. (Insert pins through all layers.) Roll remainder of quilt on right (batting and backing) so that quilt will fit under sewing machine arm. Secure roll with bicycle clips.

Attach walking foot to sewing machine and use thread to match quilt *backing*. Sew directly on stitching of row seam allowance. (Stitching attaches quilt top to quilt layers so that

it shows only on the back.) Continue in same manner for all rows.

Finished Edges
Because of the stair-step bottom edge, Katy suggests stitching a facing to it for a clean finished edge. Cut facing for bottom of quilt, 13" x 63", from backing fabric. Turn 1 long edge under ¼" to wrong side and press. With right sides facing, match raw edge of bottom (lowest) squares to raw edge of facing, as shown in Facing Diagram. Join facing to quilt, following along stair-step edge of quilt. Trim facing even with quilt. Turn facing to quilt back, clipping corners as needed, and blindstitch folded edge to backing. Bind remaining 3 sides of quilt with blue fabric.

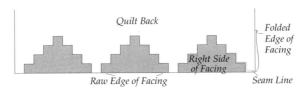

Facing Diagram

Sheri Wilkinson Lalk

Electra, Texas

Quilting is obviously a very important part of Sheri's life. Quilts can be found on every bed in her home, on many of the walls, and on the sofa. "Quilting allows me to express myself," she says, "and I only hope that I can get all of my designs made."

Sheri loves a little of every kind of quilt style and technique. That's why you'll often find a little appliqué, a little patchwork, and a little strip piecing in each one of her quilts. To achieve a successful design using a variety of techniques is not always easy. Her quilt below, *Starlight Compass*, is a example of how techniques can be mixed successfully. And her *Jacob's Fan and Flowers*, found in "Fabulous Fans," is another good example of mixed techniques.

Starlight Compass
1987

Sheri designed this quilt as she pieced it. She knew she wanted to make a compass quilt in a medallion style but that was as far as the idea went at the time. "As I pieced each section," says Sheri, "I would stop and work out the design for the next section on graph paper. I even picked out the fabrics as I went along, too."

Sheri's efforts were rewarded when *Starlight Compass* received the blue ribbon for pieced quilts at the 1987 Red River Quilters' Guild Show in Wichita Falls, Texas.

Join new sections to pieces (A) to complete compass circle. Appliqué circle (E) to center of compass. Make 5 compasses.

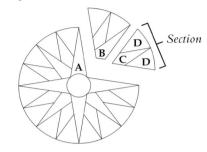

Small Compass Piecing Diagram

Center and appliqué 4 compasses to 6½" muslin squares for border corners. Trim fabric from behind compasses, leaving ¼" seam allowance. Set squares aside until border is assembled.

2. Join pieces F through I to make larger compass, as shown in Compass Piecing Diagram. Appliqué small compass to center of large compass. (See quilt photograph.)

Compass Piecing Diagram

Center and appliqué large compass to 20½" muslin square. Trim fabric from behind compass, leaving ¼" seam allowance.

3. Cut 4 strips, 1¾" x 23", from blue/rose stripe, following a printed stripe. Join to quilt and miter corners.

4. Join pieces J through M, as shown in 6" Block Piecing Diagram. Make 4 blocks.

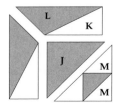

6" Block Piecing Diagram

Starlight Compass

Finished Quilt Size
79" x 79"

Fabric Requirements
Muslin	—6⅓ yd.
Tan	—2½ yd.
Rose print	—3¾ yd.★
Blue print I	—2 yd.
Blue print II	—1 yd.
Blue/rose stripe	—2 yd.★★
Backing	—5 yd.

★Includes yardage for bias binding.
★★Choose a stripe that runs length-wise with multiple stripe widths of 1¼", 1½", and 2".

Number to Cut
Template A	—20 blue print I
Template B	—20 rose print
Template C	—40 tan
Template D	—80 muslin
Template E	—5 muslin
Template F	—4 blue print I
Template G	—4 rose print
Template H	—8 tan
Template I	—16 muslin
Template J	—4 rose print
Template K	—8 muslin
Template L	—4 rose print
Template L#	—4 rose print
Template M	—4 rose print
	12 muslin
Template N	—8 blue print I
	8 rose print
	48 muslin
Template O	—8 blue print I
	8 rose print
Template P	—32 muslin
Template Q	—8 blue print I
	8 rose print
Template Q#	—8 blue print I
	8 rose print
Template R	—32 muslin
Template S	—8 blue print I
	8 rose print
Template S#	—8 blue print I
	8 rose print
Template T	—72 blue print I
	72 rose print
Template U	—140 tan
Template V	—280 muslin
Template W	—8 muslin
6½" square	—4 muslin
20½" square	—1 muslin
6⅞" square	—4 muslin
9⅜" square	—4 muslin
11½" square	—12 muslin

#Flip or turn over template if fabric is one-sided.

Quilt Top Assembly
1. Join 2 pieces (D) to sides of piece (C) to form a section, as shown in Small Compass Piecing Diagram. Make 8 sections. Join 2 sections to sides of each piece (B), as shown.

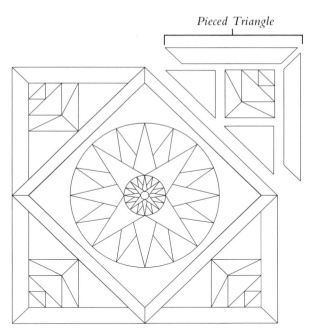

Quilt Piecing Diagram I

Quilt Piecing Diagram II

Cut 6⅞" muslin squares in half on the diagonal to make 8 triangles. Join triangles to sides of blocks, as shown in Quilt Piecing Diagram I, to make 4 pieced triangles.

Cut 8 strips, 2½" x 26½", from blue/rose stripe, following a printed stripe. Join to pieced triangles, as shown, and miter corners. Join pieced triangles to quilt and trim any excess fabric from strips to ¼" seam allowance.

5. Join pieces N through S, as shown in 8½" Block Piecing Diagram. Make 8 blocks using blue print I and muslin and 8 blocks using rose print and muslin. (See quilt photograph.)

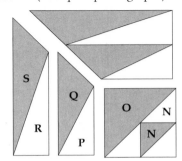

8½" Block Piecing Diagram

Cut 9⅜" muslin squares in half on the diagonal to make 8 triangles. Join triangles to sides of 4 blocks made with blue print, as shown in Triangle

Piecing Diagram, to make 4 pieced triangles. (Set aside remaining blocks. See step 8.)

Triangle Piecing Diagram

Cut 8 strips, 2" x 21", from blue/rose stripe, following a printed stripe. Join to pieced triangles, as shown, and miter corners. Trim excess fabric.

6. Cut 5 strips, 2½" wide, across fabric from blue print II. Cut 10 strips, 2½" wide, across fabric from muslin.

Join 2 muslin strips to blue print II strip lengthwise with blue print II strip in center to form a panel. Make 5 panels.

Cut 72 segments across seam lines of panels at 2½" intervals.

Stagger 9 segments and join to form a strip, as shown in Border Piecing Diagram. Make 8 strips. Trim excess fabric from strips lengthwise, as shown.

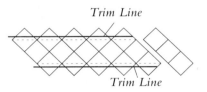

Border Piecing Diagram

Join strips to pieced triangles, as shown in Quilt Piecing Diagram II, and trim excess fabric at strip ends. Join pieced triangles to quilt.

7. Cut 4 strips, 2" wide, from blue/rose stripe, following a printed stripe. Join to quilt and miter corners.

8. Join remaining 8½" blocks to 11½" muslin squares, as shown in Large Triangle Piecing Diagram. Miter corners of muslin squares to fit, as shown. Trim across squares, leaving a ¼" seam allowance.

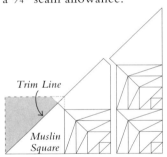

Large Triangle Piecing Diagram

Cut 8 strips, 1½" wide, from tan for sides of large triangle. Join to large triangles, as shown in Quilt Piecing Diagram III, and miter corners.

9. Cut 7 strips, 2" wide, across fabric from blue print II. Cut 14 strips, 2" wide, across fabric from muslin. Join strips lengthwise to make panels as above. (See step 6.)

Cut 136 segments across seam lines of panels at 2" intervals. Stagger segments and join, as above, to make borders. Join borders to large triangles, as shown in Quilt Piecing Diagram III. (Inset shows how to join corners. Trim excess fabric as needed.)

Cut 8 strips, 1½" wide, from tan for sides of large triangle. Join to large triangle, as shown, and miter corners. Join large triangles to quilt.

10. Join 2 pieces (V) to sides of each diamond (U), as shown in Compass Border Piecing Diagram. Join to sides of 18 blue print II triangles (T) and 18 rose print triangles (T), as shown, to make 1 pieced border. (Alternate colors of triangles, as shown.) Join triangle (W) to ends of pieced border. Make 4 pieced borders.

Quilt Piecing Diagram III

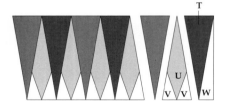

Compass Border Piecing Diagram

Join 2 pieced borders to sides of quilt. Join border corner blocks, made in step 1, to ends of remaining pieced borders. Join to quilt. (See quilt drawing.)

Round quilt corners after quilting. (See Finished Edges.)

Quilting

Outline-quilt outside seam line of all compass and border pieces. Outline-quilt ¼" inside seam line of all remaining pieces. Choose your favorite quilting pattern for open muslin areas.

Finished Edges

Mark quilt corners for a round edge and trim. Bind with rose print.

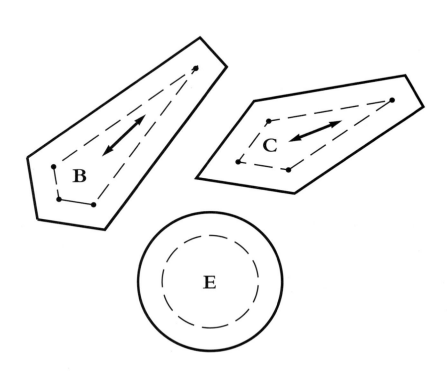

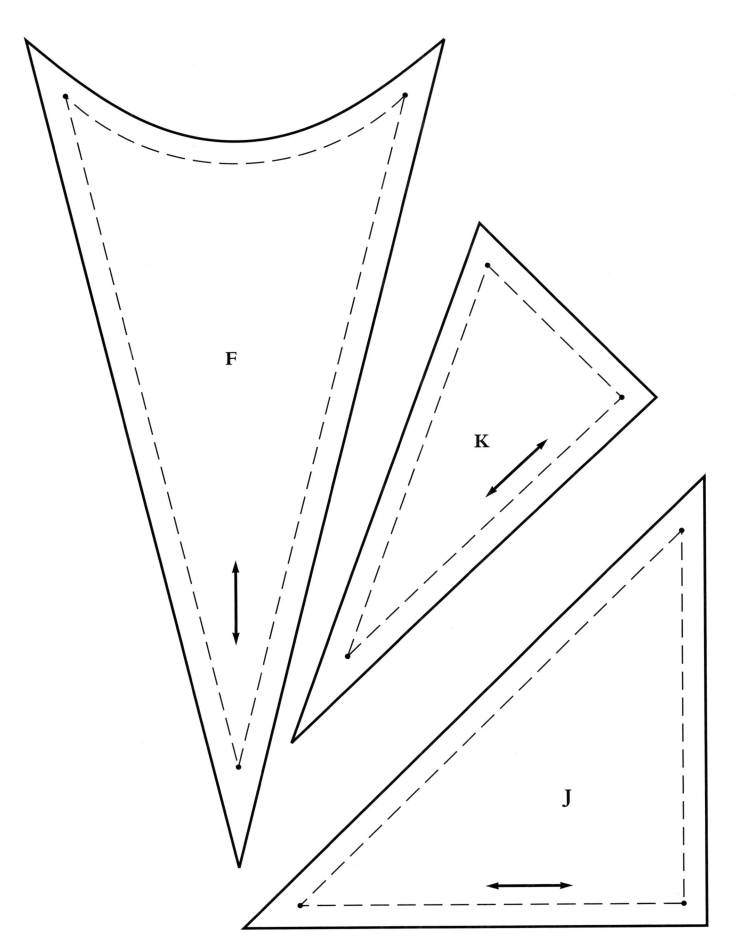

F

K

J

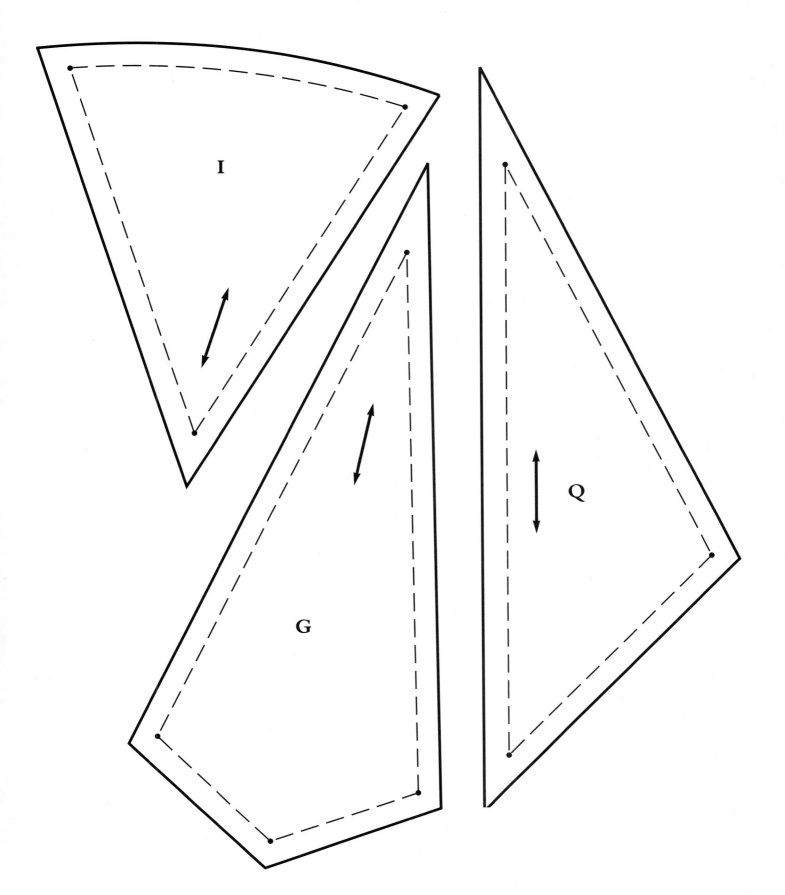

I

G

Q

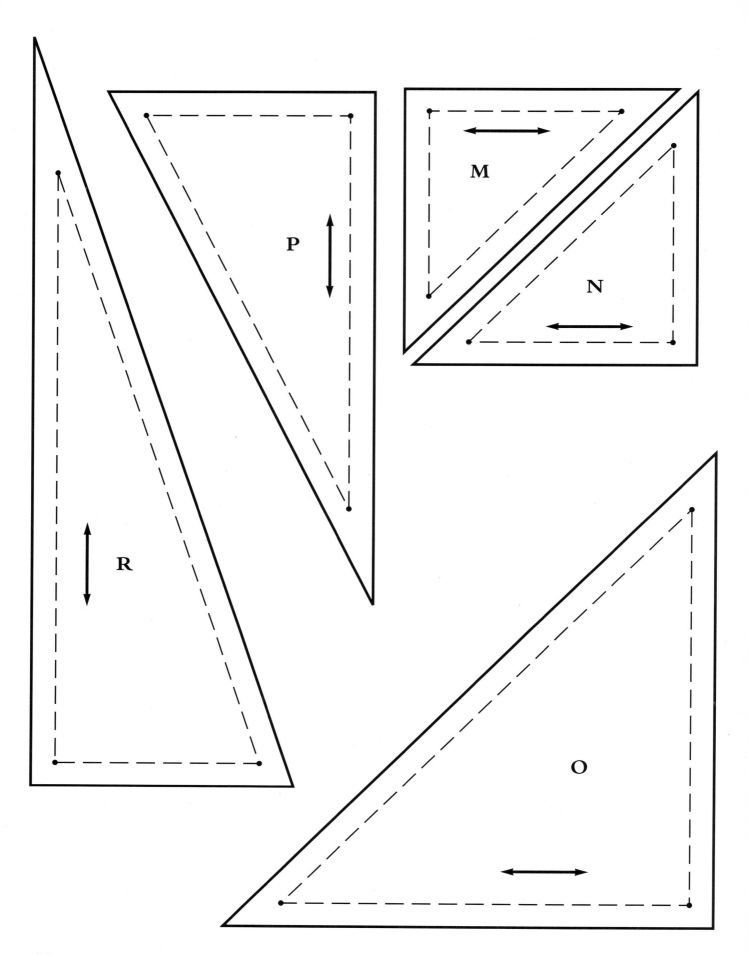

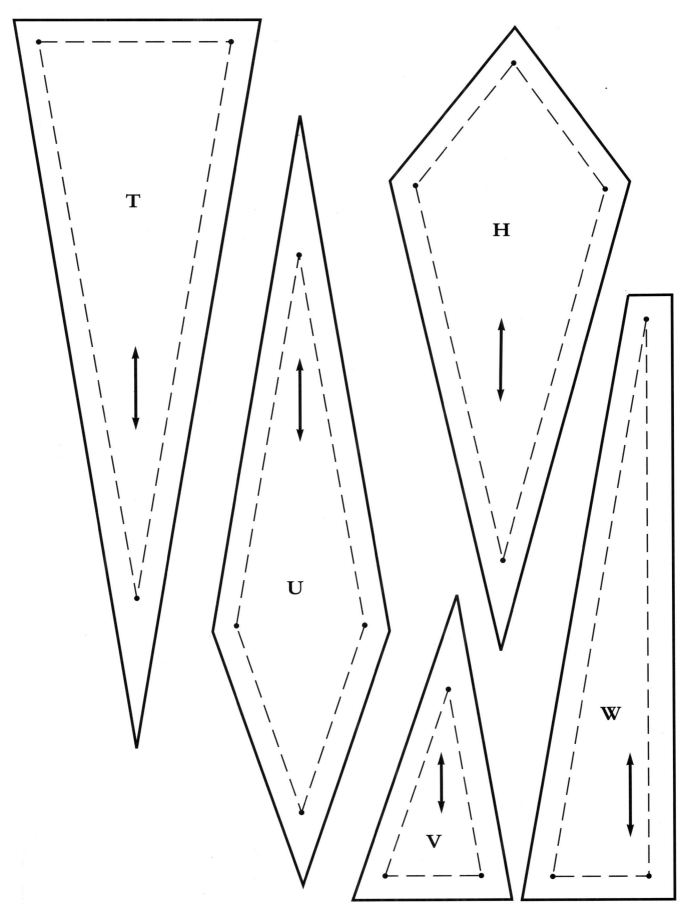

Judy Severson

Belvedere, California

A nationally recognized printmaker and quilter, Judy Severson gives all beginning quilters hope. "When I completed my first quilt," says Judy, "I told myself that I would never do it again!" But as time passed, she found a lasting pleasure in her new achievement, and within three years, she was ready to attempt her second quilt. "I did it again, and then again, and after learning to appliqué," she says, "I was hooked."

Incorporation of her printmaking and quiltmaking was the next step. She began experimenting by duplicating the designs from her embossed prints as stuffed work (trapunto) in her quilts. (See photograph below.) The marriage of the two techniques has been tremendously successful, as you can see from her *Feathers of Peace* quilt. Judy delights in reviewing her quilts, as they give her images of her own history. "I look at them as stages of my own life," she says. "They have all been slow to come, and the stitches hold together many memories."

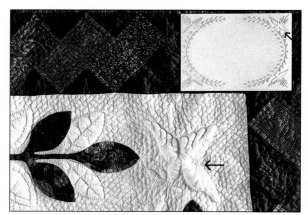

Judy took her embossed bird design (small arrow) and repeated it in trapunto on her quilt (arrow).

Feathers of Peace
1991

Challenged by a desire to make stuffed work an integral part of a quilt, Judy chose the Princess Feather pattern as her starting point. While working on the feather pattern, she discovered the breathtaking eighteenth-century medallion quilts and decided this quilt would be a medallion too.

Every part of the quilt was designed to somehow integrate stuffed work into the design. The first patchwork border was selected so that Judy could add more stuffed work, and appliquéd leaves are alternated with stuffed leaves.

Since her days are spent making unique embossed quilt prints and note cards, Judy admits that her fabric quilts are made slowly. "Because of this, they never turn out as I first design them," she says. "But I like to keep a flexible mind and incorporate ideas from quilts of the past as I learn about them."

Feathers of Peace

Approximate Finished Quilt Size
69½" x 69½"

Fabric Requirements
White	—2 yd.
Navy print I★	—1¾ yd.
Navy print II★	—¾ yd.
Navy print★★	—1½ yd.
Misc. navy prints	—2¼ yd.
Navy print for bias binding	—1¼ yd.
Backing	—4½ yd.

★For appliqués
★★For outer border triangles

Materials for Trapunto
Embroidery floss, white
Embroidery hoop, small
Orange stick or knitting needle
Stuffing, polyester
White batiste — 3 yd.

Number to Cut
Template A	— 4 navy print I
	4 navy print II
Template B	—1 navy print I
Template C	—1 navy print II
Template D	—24 white★★★
Template E	—64 misc. navy prints
Template F	—140 navy print
Template G	—68 misc. navy prints
Template H	—4 misc. navy prints
Template I	—4 navy print I

★★★Some quilters may prefer to work trapunto in squares before cutting fabric. See steps 3 and 5.

Quilt Top Assembly
1. Cut 32" square from white. Finger-crease square in half twice to find center and make guidelines. Alternate navy print I feathers (A) with navy print II feathers (A) on square, as shown in Medallion Setting Diagram and quilt photograph.

Medallion Setting Diagram

Appliqué feathers to square. Layer-appliqué centers (B and C) to feathers, as shown.

2. To prepare square for trapunto, place feather template (A) between appliquéd feathers and lightly mark around template. Mark bird design in each corner.

Cut 32" square from batiste. With raw edges aligned, baste batiste square to wrong side of appliquéd square. Using the lining method described in the "Editor's Note," work trapunto in marked feathers and birds.

3. Mark plume design on point in each square D. Work trapunto in each square. (Judy worked her initials in 3 squares.)

4. Alternate squares (D) with triangles (E) for medallion border, as shown in Medallion Setting Diagram. Make borders for sides first and join to quilt. Make borders for top and bottom, and join to quilt.

5. Cut 2 borders, 8¾" wide, from white and join to top and bottom of quilt. Cut 2 borders, 8¾" wide, from white and join to remaining sides.

Center and appliqué branch (I) to each border, as shown in quilt photograph. Prepare borders for trapunto. Work trapunto leaves between appliquéd leaves. (Embroider lines for leaf veins.) Work trapunto bird in each corner.

6. Alternate triangles (F) with rectangles (G) to make short strips. Join strips at sides to make 4 pieced borders, as shown in Border Piecing Diagram and whole quilt drawing. Join borders to quilt and join at corners with triangles (F) and square (H), as shown in diagrams.

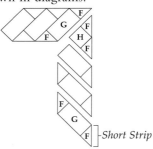

Border and Piecing Diagram

Quilting
Stipple-quilt between trapunto feathers and appliquéd feathers near feather stems. Meander-quilt inside appliquéd leaves. Background-quilt diagonal lines, ½" apart, in remainder of medallion square and squares (D). Outline-quilt ¼" inside seam lines of triangles (E).

Stipple-quilt between trapunto leaves and appliquéd leaves near stem. Background-quilt diagonal lines, ½" apart, in borders. Outline-quilt ¼" inside seam lines of leaves.

Outline-quilt ¼" inside seam lines of rectangles (G). Quilt 2 lines, ¼" apart, inside first quilting line. Outline-quilt ¼" inside seam lines of triangles (F).

Finished Edges
Bind with blue print.

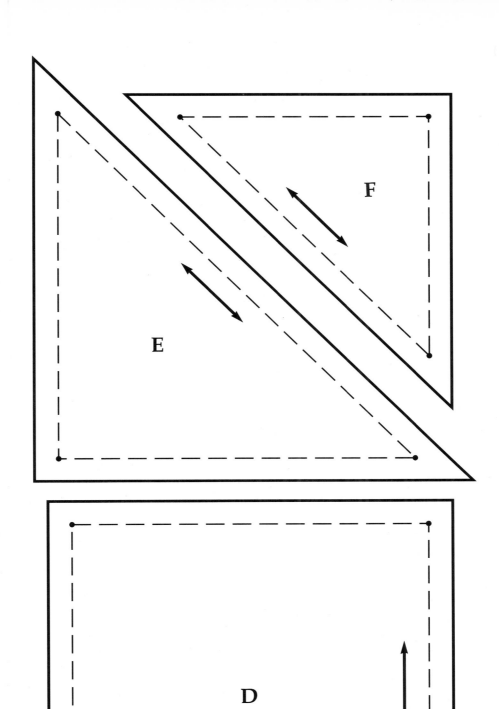

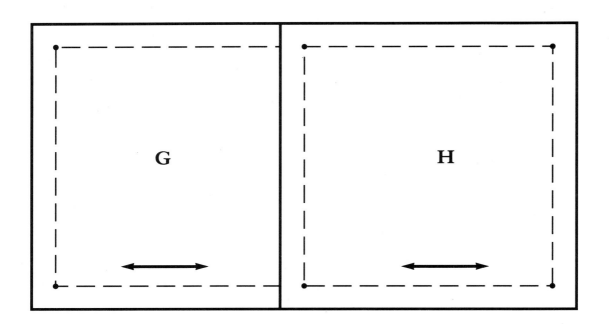

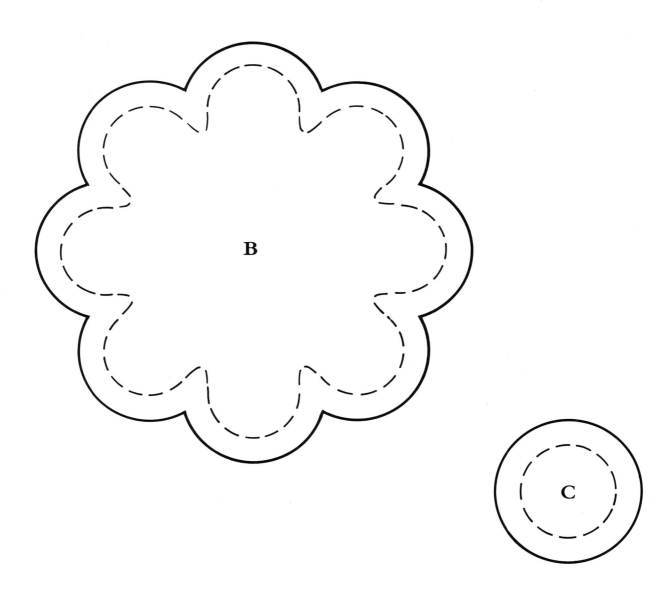

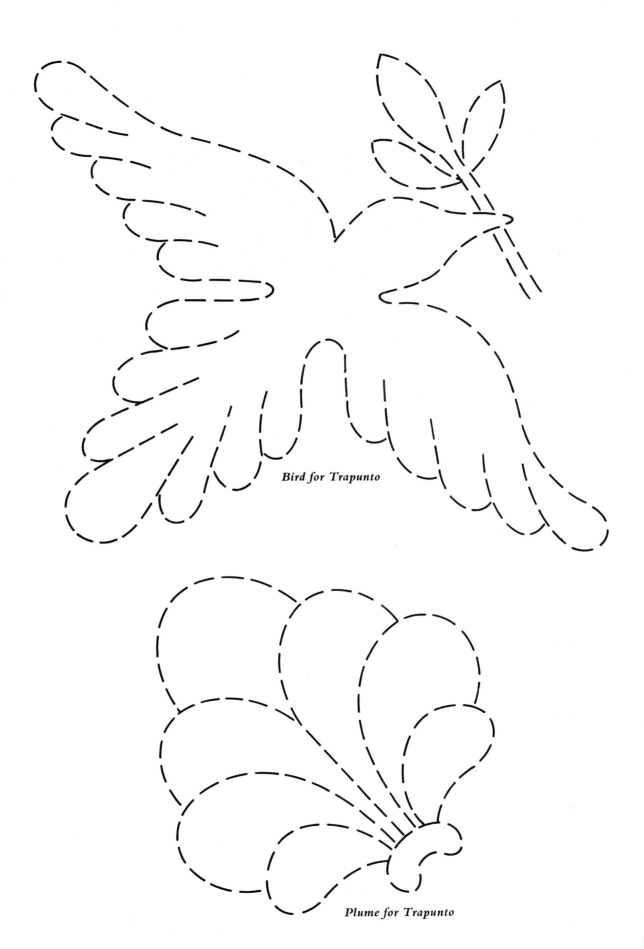

Bird for Trapunto

Plume for Trapunto

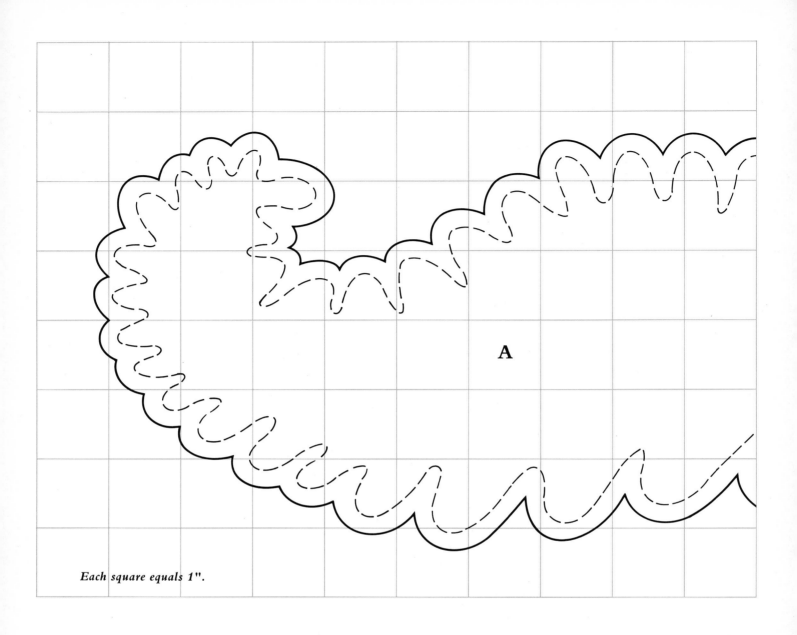

A

Each square equals 1".

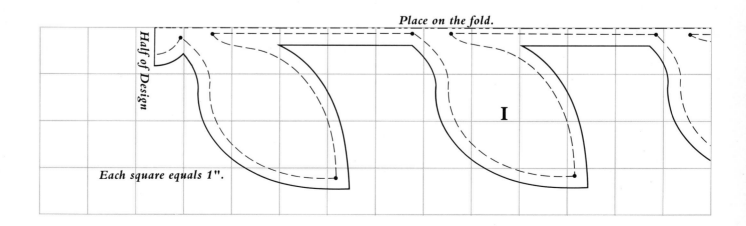

Place on the fold.

Half of Design

I

Each square equals 1".

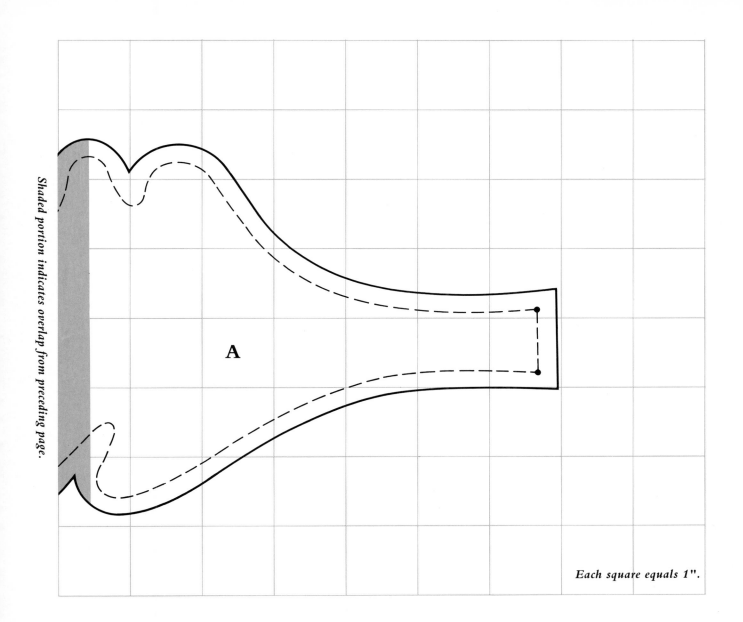

Shaded portion indicates overlap from preceding page.

A

Each square equals 1".

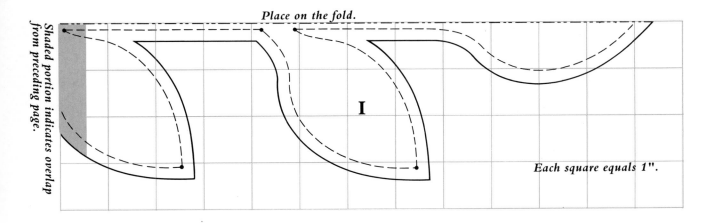

Shaded portion indicates overlap from preceding page.

Place on the fold.

I

Each square equals 1".

Debra Wagner

Hutchinson, Minnesota

"I don't make quilts to *have* quilts," says Debra. "I make quilts for the fun of designing and executing them. The more complex the design, the more I enjoy the process." Debra literally grew up playing with sewing machines in her parents' sewing machine store. "I could demonstrate the machine's features by the time I was 13 years old," she says. Therein is the root of her belief that the sewing machine needle can do anything a hand-held needle can do. This philosophy has stimulated her to write books on sewing machine artistry (see *Winter Bouquet*) and has motivated her to perfect newer methods for transferring all types of traditional hand-needlework techniques to machine.

Quiltmaking for Debra matches her interests in two very unique ways. "One, unlike other textile arts," says Debra, "quiltmaking attracts a large well-organized following. Second, quiltmaking gives me a creative outlet that can reflect any era or style."

Indiana Rose
1990
Let Debra Wagner introduce you to the world of appli-quilting as you make *Indiana Rose*. Appli-quilting is a one-step process of appliquéing and quilting by machine that cuts your quiltmaking time in half. Un-appliquéd, block-size squares are first prepared for quilting. Pattern pieces are then machine-appliquéd through all layers with a very tiny satin stitch. (See close-up photograph.) By using spooled thread to match appliqué pieces and bobbin thread to match backing, smooth appliqué stitches (satin stitches) anchor the pieces on the front, while producing uniform stitches on the back that look like machine-quilting stitches.

Debra recommends a thin, low-loft batting to keep this wall hanging soft and give it an antique look.

Indiana Rose

Finished Quilt Size
42" x 42"

Number of Blocks and Finished Size
9 blocks—9" x 9"

Fabric Requirements
Cream print	—1 yd.
Pink print	—½ yd.
Blue print	—½ yd.
Navy print	—½ yd.
Green print	—⅞ yd.
Border stripe★	—1½ yd.★★
Backing	—2½ yd.

★Choose a border stripe design with a 7½"-wide repeat.
★★Use 1 stripe from fabric for straight-of-grain binding. Depending on border stripe design, additional yardage may be necessary.

Other Materials
Appliqué foot for sewing machine
Fusible web, paper-backed, 2½ yd.
Machine embroidery threads
  to match appliqués, border,
  and backing fabrics
Safety pins, 5 dozen,
  brass or nickel, size 1
Spray starch
Tracing paper

Number to Cut‡
Template A	—12 pink print
	12 blue print
	12 navy print
Template B	—36 green print
Template C	—3 pink print
	3 blue print
	3 navy print
Template D	—9 green print

‡ See step 3 before cutting fabrics.

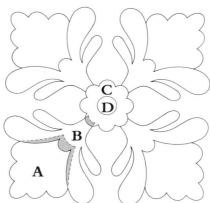

Placement Diagram

Quilt Assembly
1. Spray-starch cream print and cut nine 9½" squares (blocks).

Make a full-size master placement pattern of block by using pattern pieces and tracing paper. (See Placement Diagram.) Lightly trace pattern on each block.

2. Spray-starch backing fabric and cut nine 10" squares. Cut nine 10" squares from batting.

3. Press fusible web to back of all appliqué fabrics. Do not remove paper. Trace appliqué patterns (A through D) on paper side of web. Cut out pieces on solid cutting line. (Shaded portions on patterns indicate the part of the fabric that will be covered by another fabric [lapped edges].)

4. Remove paper from flowers (A) and press in place on each block. (See quilt photograph for color arrangement.) Next press leaves (B), followed by central flower (C) and center (D).

5. Layer each block for machine appli-quilting. Safety-pin layers together, placing pins about every 3", especially around edges of blocks. Place pins only in the background fabric and not in appliqué design. (Placing them in the design will interfere with machine stitching.)

6. Thread machine with spooled thread to match flower (A) fabric and bobbin thread to match backing fabric. Set stitch width for a narrow zigzag stitch (1.55 mm to 2 mm). Set stitch length for a satin stitch. (If your machine has tension adjustment for making buttonholes, use those settings.) Stitch around raw edges of flowers. Do not stitch on lapped edges.

7. Follow same procedure for leaves (B), central flower (C), and center (D), changing spooled thread as required. Stitch in same sequence as pieces were layered.

8. Trim batting and backing of all blocks to 9½" square. Arrange blocks in 3 rows of 3 blocks each, as shown in quilt photograph.

To join, fold back backing and batting of adjacent blocks to expose top (appliquéd) layer of fabric, as shown in Block Joining Diagram I, and pin. With right sides facing and raw edges aligned, join top layers of blocks at sides to form a row. Press all seams of each row in one direction.

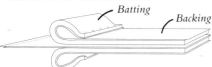

Block Joining Diagram I

Unpin backing and batting and trim batting so that edges abut. Overlap backing, turn one side of backing under ¼", and slipstitch to backing and batting only. (See Block Joining Diagram II.) Join rows in same manner.

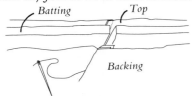

Block Joining Diagram II

9. For backing border, cut 2 borders, 8" x 45", and 2 borders, 8" x 27½", from backing fabric. (Backing border is sewn to quilt before quilt top border and is not mitered.)

With right sides facing and raw edges aligned, join short borders to top and bottom of quilt backing only. (Do not stitch through all layers.) Join remaining backing borders to opposite sides.

10. For quilt top borders, cut 4 borders, 8" x 45", from border stripe. With right sides facing and raw edges aligned, join borders to quilt top only and miter corners.

11. Cut 2 strips of batting, 8" x 45", and 2 strips, 8" x 27½".

Turn back quilt top border and backing border on 1 side to expose seam allowances and batting of inner quilt. Secure short batting strip to quilt body (seam allowances and batting) with a whipstitch. Repeat on opposite side. Secure long batting strips to remaining sides.

Turn borders back to correct position and safety-pin layers together.

12. Using a straight stitch, machine-quilt border layers together, following stripes and designs.

Finishing

Trim batting and backing even with quilt top. Zigzag-stitch around quilt edge with your widest and longest zigzag stitch.

Cut 2"-wide straight-of-grain binding strips from 1 stripe in border fabric. Fold strips lengthwise to make a double binding and bind quilt.

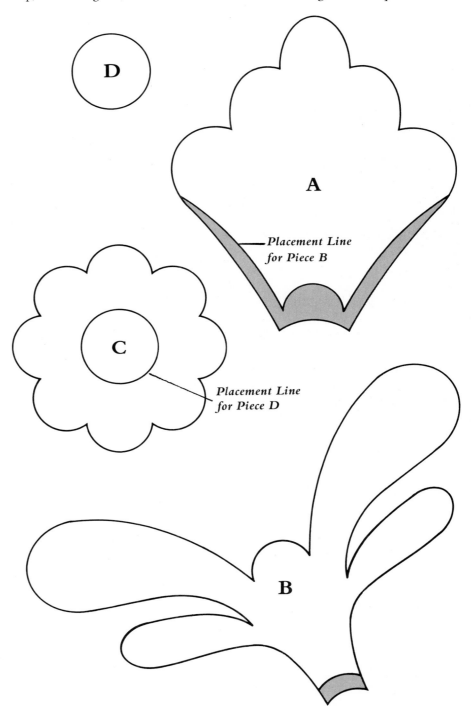

89

Winter Bouquet
1989

Debra keeps telling people that *Winter Bouquet* was machine-quilted. "But even when they are standing in front of it, they argue with me that it wasn't!" says Debra. The reason for the argument may be that Debra is an expert at machine quilting. She has co-authored a book on machine embroidery, *Wagner's Sewing Machine Artistry*, and *Winter Bouquet* was the quilt used to demonstrate machine-quilting techniques in the Singer Sewing Company's book, *Quilting by Machine*. (See "Resources" for details.)

Trapunto for *Winter Bouquet* can be executed after machine quilting in one of three ways. (See step 7.) For large projects, Debra's choice is to use a commercial machine that injects wisps of fiber to fill the space. No matter which method of trapunto you use, Debra believes that the best results for this project are obtained by using the correct batting. "The batt must be very thin to accept the heavy stipple quilting," says Debra, "and to accentuate the trapunto." (She recommends taking a 100-percent cotton batt and splitting its layer in two to get a super-thin batting layer.)

Winter Bouquet won first place in the Other Techniques, Professional or Amateur category at the 5th Annual American Quilter's Society Show, Paducah, Kentucky, in 1989; it also appeared in the *'90 American Quilter's Society Calendar*. (See "Resources.")

This quilt is not recommended for beginners.

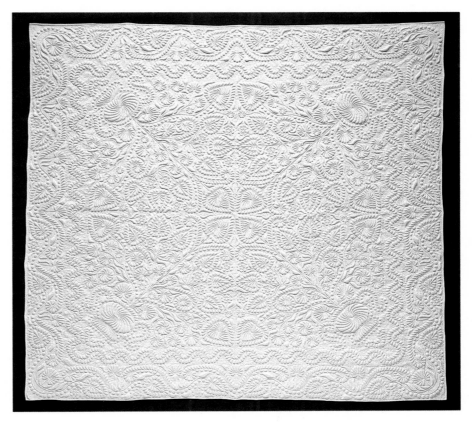

Winter Bouquet

Finished Quilt Size
90" x 94½"

Fabric Requirements★
Muslin, bleached   —3 yd.
Muslin, bleached
  for bias binding   —1 yd.
Muslin, bleached
  for backing   —3 yd.
★Requirements are based on 108"-wide, 100% cotton fabric.

Other Materials
Awl★★
Bicycle clips
Crochet hook, small★★
Darning foot for sewing machine
Freezer paper
Marker, black permanent
Safety pins, 5 dozen,
  brass or nickel, size 1
Stuffing, polyester or acrylic yarn★★
Tapestry needle★★
White machine embroidery thread,
  10 spools (300 yd./spool)
★★See step 7.

Quilt Assembly
1. Wash quilt top fabric (3 yd. of muslin) in hot water to shrink it. (If using colored or print fabric, wash it in warm water.)

(The quilt, and therefore the quilt backing fabric [muslin], is washed after machine-quilting. [See step 6.] This shrinks the backing fabric for the first time and results in the quilted top being a little larger than the backing. Because of this, unquilted spaces on the quilt top puff up. The joy of this step is that the puffing makes stuffing these spaces easier. In addition, once stuffed, these puffed areas are even more pronounced because the fabric threads have been relaxed by the washing.)

2. Referring to the Quilting Diagram for Quarter of Quilt, make a full-size master quilting pattern for a quarter of the quilt. (Debra uses large sheets of freezer paper taped together for her master pattern.)

Use black permanent marker to trace quilting patterns and center point because the master pattern will need to be flipped.

3. Fold quilt top in quarters and lightly mark center. Open quilt top and place master quilting pattern under lower right-hand quarter of quilt top. Match center of quilt top to center point of master. Safety-pin fabric to master in several locations to stabilize it. Lightly trace quilting patterns on quilt top. Repeat for all quarters, flipping master for 2 quarters to complete pattern, as shown in quilt photograph.

4. Layer quilt for machine-quilting. Starting in center, safety-pin layers together, placing pins about 4" apart in the background areas only. (Placing them in the design will interfere with machine quilting.)

Fold or roll quilt edges inward so that you can begin machine-quilting in center of quilt top and the quilt will fit under the arm of the sewing machine. Stabilize roll with bicycle clips. (Placing a table behind your sewing machine will help support the weight of the quilt while stitching.)

Before stitching, make directional stitching diagrams for each motif to lessen the number of times stitching has to be stopped and restarted.

5. Attach darning foot to machine and lower feed dogs. Set sewing machine for darning.

Begin in center and stitch motifs first. When adjacent motifs are complete, stipple-quilt background between them. (See page 6 for information on machine stipple quilting.) Continue working from center outward.

6. Wash quilt in clear tepid water to remove markings and shrink backing.

7. For trapunto as shown in quilt photographs, use 1 of 3 methods:

1) Make a small hole with awl in backing and push wisps of stuffing into space with a small crochet hook.

2) Thread a tapestry needle with yarn and carefully insert threaded needle through fabric into space. Bring needle back out through fabric, leaving yarn in space. Gently, push yarn ends into space with needle. Repeat process until space is completely filled with yarn.

3) Use a machine that injects the stuffing into the space.

Finishing

Wash quilt again to erase all evidence of the stuffing process. Lay quilt on large flat surface to dry. Roughly square up sides and corners of wet quilt. ("Think of this step as the blocking step for your quilt," says Debra.)

After air-drying quilt, square up sides and corners once again but this time use a ruler and cut away excess fabric. Bind with double bias binding.

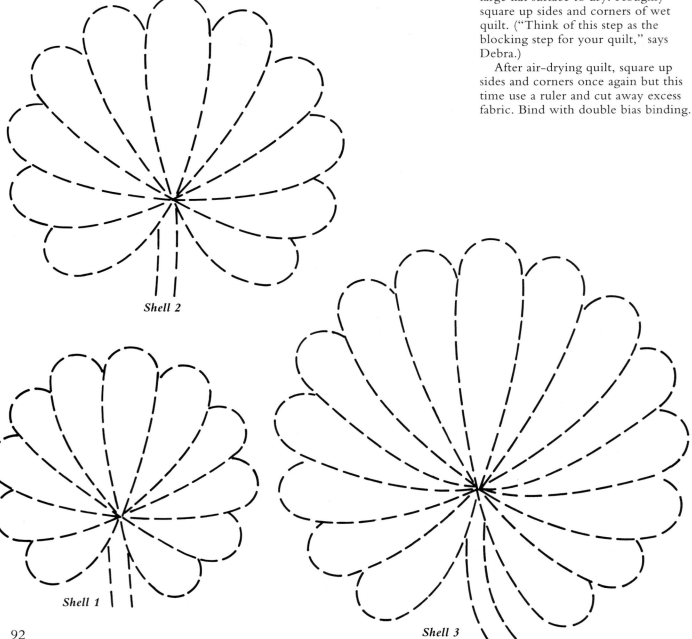

Shell 2

Shell 1

Shell 3

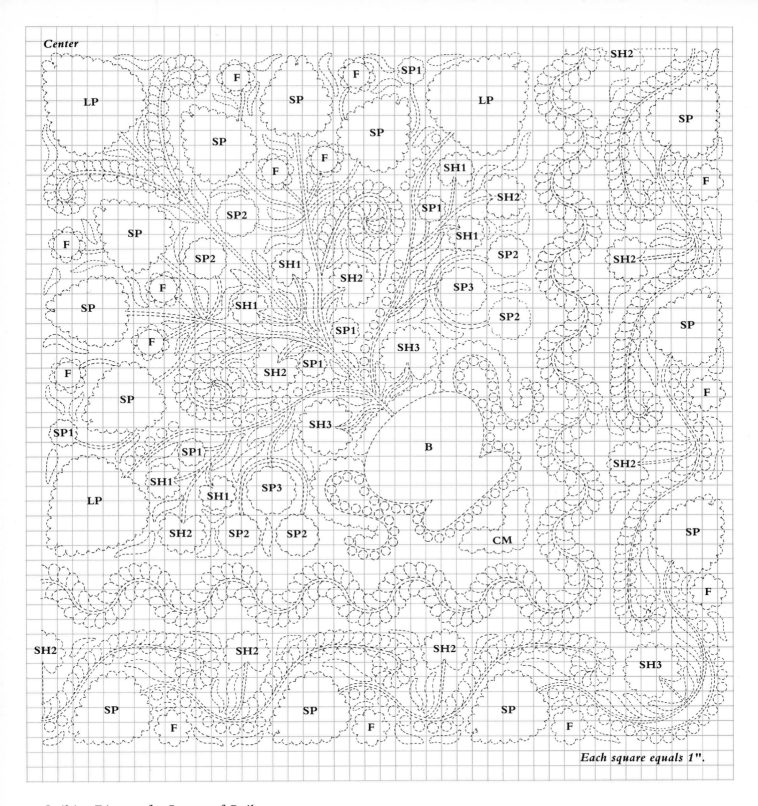

Center

Each square equals 1".

Quilting Diagram for Quarter of Quilt

Basket (B) *Shell 1 (SH1)*
Corner Motif (CM) *Shell 2 (SH2)*
Flower (F) *Shell 3 (SH3)*

Pineapple, Large (LP) *Spiral 1 (SP1)*
Pineapple, Small (SP) *Spiral 2 (SP2)*
  Spiral 3 (SP3)

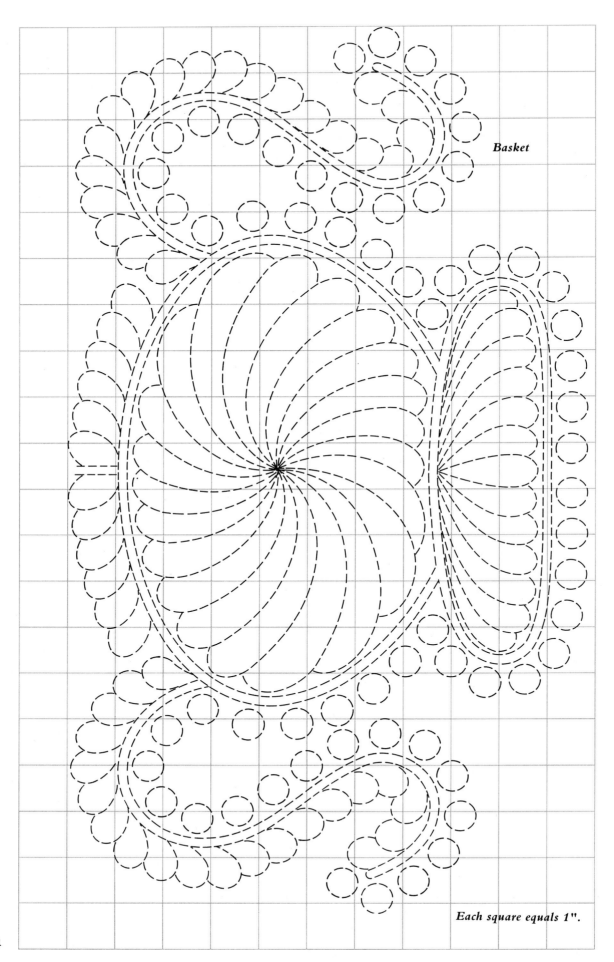

Basket

Each square equals 1".

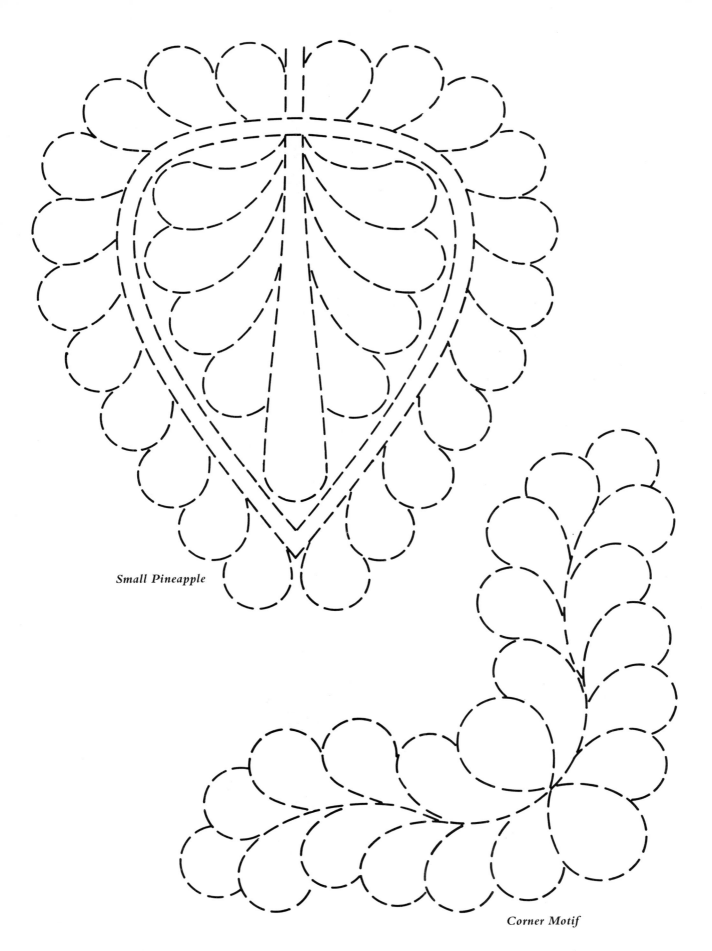

Small Pineapple

Corner Motif

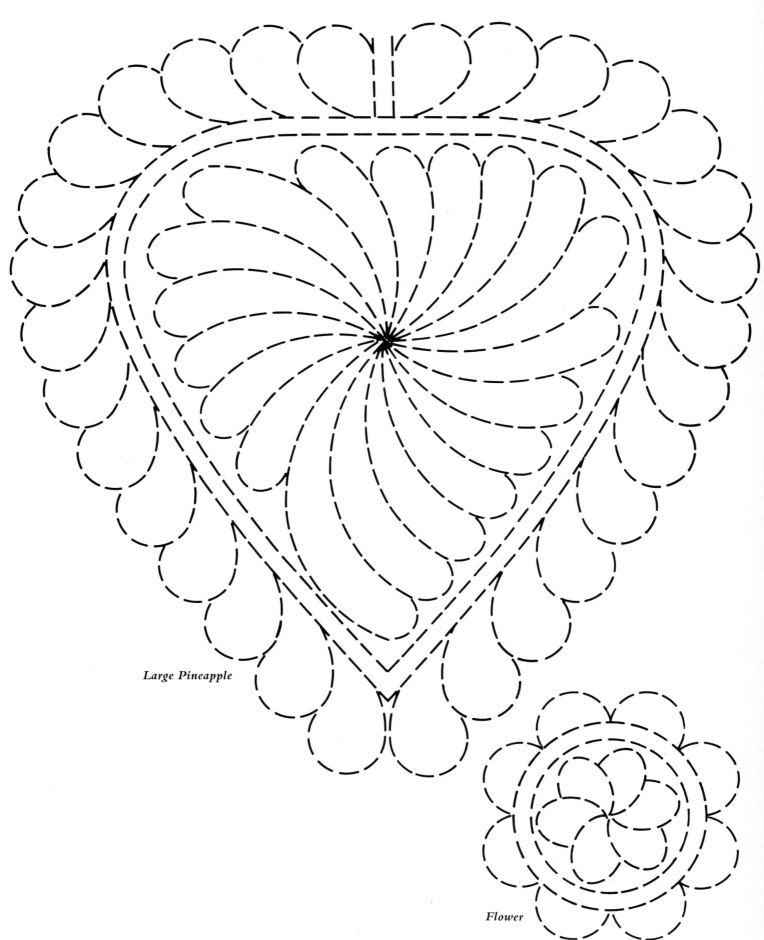

Large Pineapple

Flower

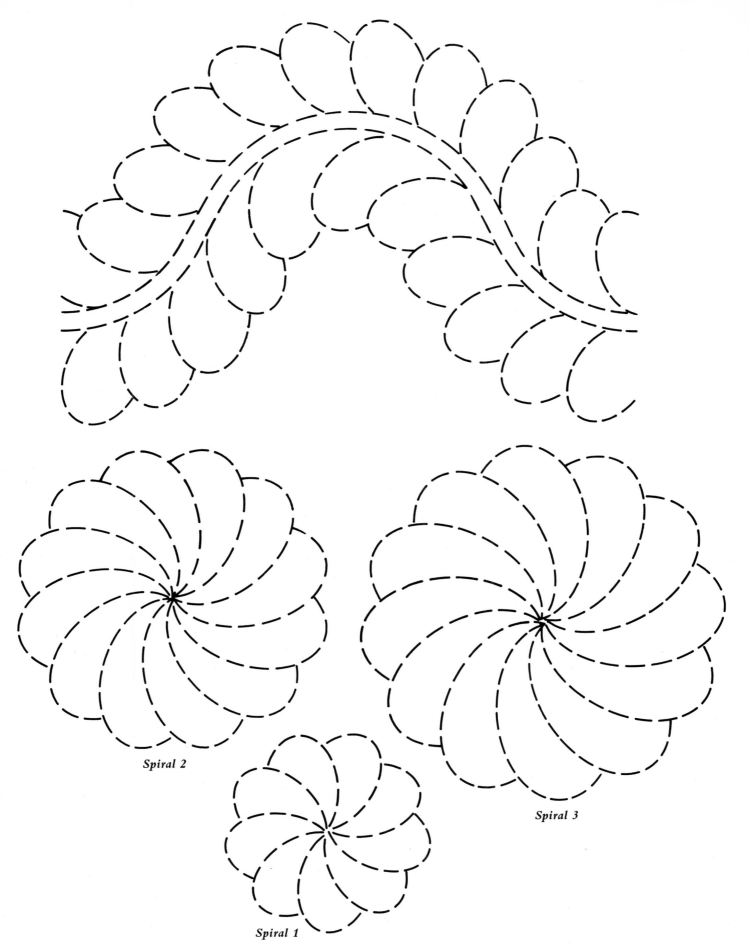

Spiral 2

Spiral 1

Spiral 3

As a professional artist and quilter, Jeanne's reasons for making quilts are no different from those of the non-professional. "I see quilting as a way to express my thoughts and ideas," she says. "My art is very much a part of me. I do it because I have to."

The times when quiltmaking is just plain hard work, Jeanne believes, are offset by other times when stitching offers time to reflect—"a sort of mini-vacation for the mind."

Learn how to enhance a traditional pattern by making Jeanne's fan quilt, found in "Fabulous Fans."

Jeanne Benson
Columbia, Maryland

Healthy Snack
1990

A drawing by Jeanne's young daughter Emily is now a fabric wall hanging. Inspired by the simplicity of a child's drawing, Jeanne saw a way to duplicate it in fabric to make a keepsake. The simple shapes are cut from fabric, machine-appliquéd to a background, and embellished with free-motion machine stitching.

Jeanne has made several of these collages and uses them as examples when she conducts her workshops at the Montpelier Cultural Arts Center in Laurel, Maryland.

Since you will want to use your own drawing to make your keepsake, our instructions give you a general supply list and guidelines for making a fabric collage.

Healthy Snack

Fabric Requirements
16" x 18" rectangle of
  unbleached canvas duck,
  medium weight
Fusible web, paper-backed, 1 yd.
Fabrics (100% cotton) for your design,
  backing, and binding

Other Materials★
Black quilting thread
Drawing with simple shapes,
  approximately 9" x 12"
Dressmaker's tracing paper and
  tracing wheel
Machine embroidery thread to
  match fabrics
Tracing paper
★See Ways to Embellish Your Keep-
sake, below.

Keepsake Assembly
1. Place tracing paper on drawing and
trace design and child's signature with
pencil.
2. Flip tracing over and place fusible
web (paper side up) on it. Trace each
shape separately onto paper side of
fusible web. Note sections of shapes
that will be under other shapes when
appliquéd and add ¼" seam allowance
to those sections only. (Those sections that do not overlap others will
not have seam allowances.)
3. Cut out shapes drawn on web and
following manufacturer's instructions,
press to wrong side of fabrics. Cut out
fabric shapes.
4. Peel off paper backing, position
shapes on background canvas, and
press in place with a warm, dry iron.
5. Machine-appliqué shapes to background. For Emily's keepsake, Jeanne
used a ¹⁄₁₆"-wide, 18-stitch-length
zigzag stitch in a thread color coordinated to each fabric. Details in black
thread were added with free-motion
machine straight-stitching, using a
darning foot and lowered feed dogs.
6. For child's signature, use dressmaker's tracing paper and a tracing
wheel. Place dressmaker's tracing paper between tracing paper with signature and background fabric. Trace
along signature lines with wheel to
make a dotted line to stitch over.
(Jeanne used the same stitch width
and length she used above.)

Emily Benson's Original Drawing

Machine-Quilting
Layer keepsake using a thin batting.
Jeanne framed Emily's drawing with
the same zigzag stitch used above and
then with a decorative stitch, made
½" from the zigzag stitching.

Finished Edges
Bind with 1½"-wide binding strips
and miter corners. Add a hanging
sleeve to back or set keepsake in a
frame.

WAYS TO EMBELLISH YOUR KEEPSAKE

★Beads, buttons, lace, ribbons, and trims
★Rubber or homemade stamps for stamping words or designs
★Fine point permanent markers for adding details. (Heat-set
  any marks with an iron.)

TRADITIONS
IN
QUILTING

Jean Briggs

Gambier, Ohio

"My friends tell me I have a thing for putting teeny-tiny pieces together," says Jean. Hand-piecing is Jean's favorite part of quilt-making, and her teeny-tiny pieces easily tag along on family trips for quick assembly on the road.

As you would expect, her first quilt contained small pieces—a Grandmother's Flower Garden that she made when she was in junior high school. "I started sewing when I was 12," she says. "My love for sewing, for choosing fabrics, patterns, and colors was a natural foundation for my interest in quilting." Jean is an active member of Knox County Quilters' Guild of Mt. Vernon, Ohio.

Pinwheel
1989

Triangles of color in Jean's *Pinwheel* flicker at passersby like fireflies on a hot summer evening. Your eyes dart from one spot, to another, to another, and then to another, as its surface coaxes you on a quilt exploration.

Pieced and quilted entirely by hand, Jean's quilt offers you a chance to exhaust your scrap pile. This design of scrap Pinwheel blocks was taken from an antique quilt Jean spied at a quilt show. To give the set some focus, Jean placed a rectangle of blue print Pinwheel blocks outside a rectangle of red print Pinwheel blocks.

Pinwheel

Finished Quilt Size
80" x 107½"

Number of Blocks and Finished Size
1,376 Pinwheel blocks—2½" x 2½"

Fabric Requirements
Red prints	—1⅞ yd.
Blue prints	—2¼ yd.
Dk. prints★	—7¼ yd. total
Lt./med. prints★	—7¼ yd. total
Blue for bias binding	—1¼ yd.
Backing	—6¼ yd.

★May select red and blue prints also. The fabric requirements for red and blue prints above are for the red and blue print Pinwheel blocks in the red and blue rectangles and borders. See step 1.

Number to Cut★★
Square	—484 red prints
	596 blue prints
	2,212 dk. prints
	2,212 lt/med. prints

★★Fabric squares are cut diagonally into 2 triangles. See step 1.

Quilt Top Assembly
1. Group squares from 1 blue print and 1 red print into sets of 4 to make 142 sets of 2 blue and 2 red print squares each. Make 78 sets of 2 squares each from 2 blue prints. Make 50 sets of 2 squares each from 2 red prints. Each set will make 1 Pinwheel block.

Group remaining squares in same manner from 1 dk. print and 1 lt./med. print into 1,106 sets.

2. Cut each square in half diagonally to make 2 triangles. (Keep triangles in their set.)

With right sides facing and raw edges aligned, join contrasting triangles from each set to form triangle-squares, as shown in Block Piecing Diagram. Join triangle-squares to

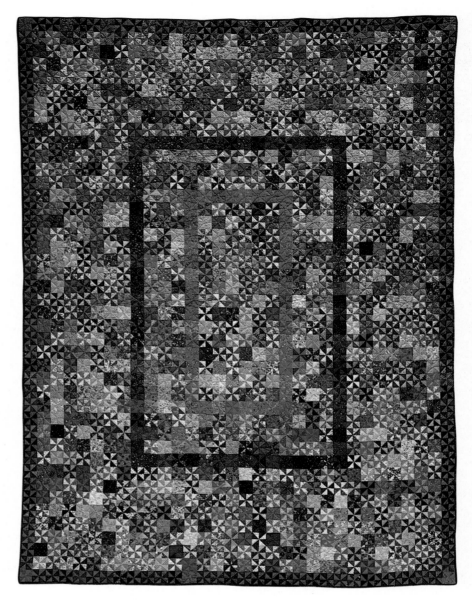

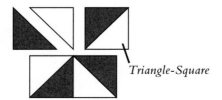

Triangle-Square

Block Piecing Digram

complete block. Repeat for each set to make a total of 1,376 blocks.

3. Refer to quilt photograph and arrange blocks in 43 rows of 32 blocks each. Note placement of blue and red print Pinwheel blocks on outside edges and red print Pinwheel blocks on quilt corners.

Join blocks at sides to form rows and join rows.

Quilting
Outline-quilt outside seam lines of alternate triangles.

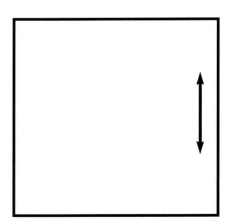

Finished Edges
Bind with blue fabric.

"Time flies when you are hand-piecing," says Mary. "I am so grateful to my daughter for getting me to try quilting. She kept encouraging me—'You can do it mom, you can do it.'"

Since then, Mary learned how important quilting had become to her when she had to have hip replacement surgery. "It was my quilting projects that helped to carry me through the difficult convalescent period," says Mary.

Mary Conover
West Simsbury, Connecticut

Hollyhock
1989

Floral wreaths have been popular with American quilters since the nineteenth century, and there's a good chance that they will remain popular on into the next one. Mary's variation of the traditional Hollyhock Wreath adds four buds to the ring. "I have always admired red and green quilts," says Mary, "and since my daughter loves hollyhocks, I thought this was the perfect design to make for her."

Mary and her daughter, Margaret Morley, work on many quilting projects together, and this one was no exception. After Mary appliquéd each wreath and assembled the quilt, Margaret hand-quilted it with an allover cross-hatching pattern.

Hollyhock

Finished Quilt Size
75½" x 89"

Number of Blocks and Finished Size
30 blocks—13½" x 13½"

Fabric Requirements
Muslin★ —5⅞ yd.
Green —4¼ yd.
Red print —1⅝ yd.
Yellow print —½ yd.
Muslin for
  bias binding —1¼ yd.
Backing —5¼ yd.
★See steps 1, 4, and 5 before cutting muslin.

Number to Cut
Template A —120 red print
Template B —120 yellow print
Template C★★—240 green
Template D —120 red print
Template E★★—120 green
★★See step 6 before cutting pieces.

Quilt Top Assembly
1. Set aside muslin for borders. (See steps 4 and 5.) Cut thirty 14" squares (blocks) from remaining muslin. Finger-crease squares in half twice to find center and to form guidelines for appliqué.
2. Cut 30 bias strips, 1⅛" x 27", from green for wreaths.

Center and pin 1 bias strip to muslin square to make wreath that is 8½" in diameter from outside edge. Appliqué in place. (Finished width of strip is ⅝".)

Arrange pieces around wreath, as shown in Placement Diagram. Layer-appliqué pieces in place. (Numbers in parentheses in Placement Diagram indicate order for appliquéing.) Appliqué 30 blocks.

3. Arrange blocks into 6 rows of 5 blocks each. Join blocks at sides to form rows and join rows.
4. Cut 2 borders, 4½" wide, from muslin for top and bottom of quilt. Join to quilt.
5. Cut 2 borders, 4½" wide, from muslin for sides of quilt. Join to quilt.
6. Cut 2 border strips, 1⅛" wide, from green for top and bottom borders. (See quilt photograph.)

Appliqué border strips 1½" from inner quilt seam, as shown in Border Diagram.

Cut 2 border strips, 1⅛" wide, from green for sides of quilt. Appliqué border strips 1½" from inner quilt seam. Overlap border strips at corners.

Quilting
Outline-quilt outside seam lines of all appliqué pieces, including border strips. Background-quilt remainder of quilt in a 1" cross-hatching grid.

Finished Edges
Bind with muslin.

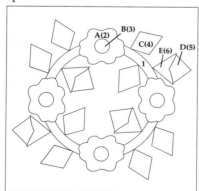

Placement Diagram

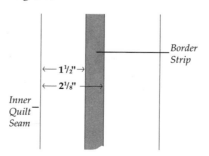

Border Diagram

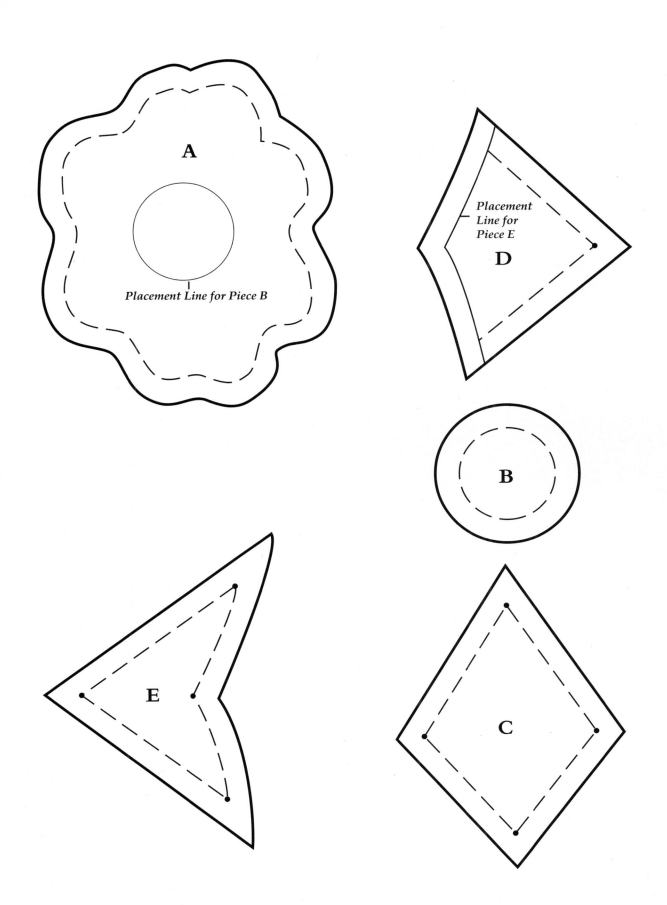

A

Placement Line for Piece B

Placement Line for Piece E

D

B

E

C

Mary Ann Keathley
Jacksonville, Arkansas

"The quilting seed was planted in me as I watched my mother and grandmothers quilt," says Mary. While growing up on a farm in northern Arkansas, Mary learned that quiltmaking was a regular part of the household chores. Quilts were needed for bedcovers, and it was the responsibility of the women on the farm to make them. This atmosphere not only motivated Mary, as a young girl, to piece a few tops of her own, but from it sparked a love of quilting that has stayed with Mary throughout her life.

"I feel most fortunate to own the quilts that my mother, and grandmothers made, and even a few made by my aunts," says Mary. "I treasure them dearly."

Mary has another quilt in "Fabulous Fans." Take a look at what can be done with a Grandmother's Fan block.

Hidden Circles
1989

When someone spends long hours to achieve a goal, the satisfaction upon completion is often much greater. That is probably why Mary calls this her favorite quilt.

She first saw a quilt made from a pattern similar to *Hidden Circles* in a book of antique quilts and knew that she had to try to make one. Since the name of that pattern was unknown to her, Mary drafted her own and then began a search for just the right fabrics. The quilt she saw had plain setting blocks between the pieced blocks, but she was not pleased with any fabric that she found for these. Instead, Mary pieced more blocks and arranged them in a block-to-block set. "It changed the entire look of the quilt," she says. "Looking closely, circles emerged; and hence, I named it *Hidden Circles*."

Hidden Circles has been exhibited at several national shows. It won first place in the scrap category at 1990 Silver Dollar City Quilt Show in Missouri, and in the same year won blue and viewers' choice ribbons at the Arkansas Quilters' Guild Show.

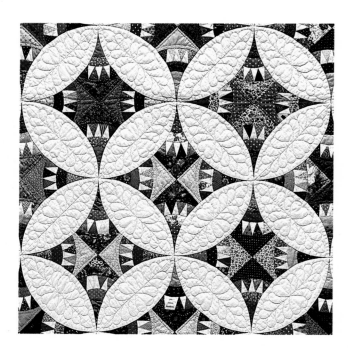

Quilt Top Assembly

1. Join pieces A through F to form a unit, as shown in Block Piecing Diagram I.

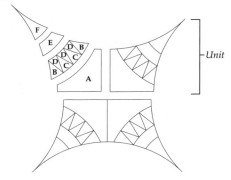

Block Piecing Diagram I

Make 4 units for each block. Join 2 units at sides of piece As to form a section, as shown. Make 2 sections and join sections. Join piece Gs to sides of units, as shown in Block Piecing Diagram II. Make 32 blocks.

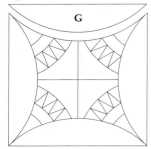

Block Piecing Diagram II

2. Join pieces A through F and H to form a pieced square, as shown in Setting Triangle Piecing Diagram. Join 2 triangles (I) to sides of square to form a triangle, as shown. Make 14 pieced setting triangles.

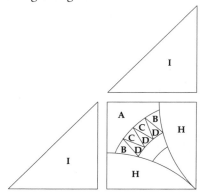

Setting Triangle Piecing Diagram

Hidden Circles

Finished Quilt Size
84" x 101"

Number of Blocks and Finished Size
32 blocks—12" x 12"

Fabric Requirements
Muslin .   —8 yd.
Scraps   —5 yd. total
Print★   —3⅛ yd.
Green print   —1¾ yd.
Rust   —⅛ yd.
Lt. rust   —⅛ yd.
Backing   —6 yd.
★Includes yardage for border flowers, appliquéd border strip, and bias binding.

Number to Cut
Template A   —142 scraps
Template B   —142 scraps
Template B★★—142 scraps
Template C   —284 scraps
Template D   —426 muslin★★★
Template E   —142 scraps
Template F   —142 scraps
Template G   —132 muslin★★★
Template H   —14 muslin★★★
Template H★★—14 muslin★★★
Template I   —28 muslin★★★
Template J   —24 print
Template K   —6 rust
Template L   —6 lt. rust
Template M   —10 green print#
Template M★★—10 green print#
Template N   —8 green print#
Template N★★—8 green print#
Template O   —16 green print#
Template P   —16 print
★★Flip or turn over template if fabric is one-sided.
★★★See step 4 before cutting fabric.
#See step 5 before cutting fabric.

Other Materials
¼" and ½" metal bias bars

3. Join blocks at sides to form diagonal rows, as shown in Setting Diagram I. Add piece Gs to 1 end of 2 rows as shown. Make 2 corner units. Join rows and corner units.

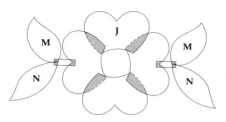

Border Flower Piecing Diagram

Position flower petals (J) and stems at corners and sides of border and layer-appliqué, as shown in Border Flower Piecing Diagram. Layer-appliqué flower centers (K and L) to petals (J).

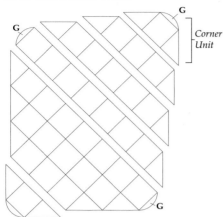

Setting Diagram I

4. Cut 4 borders, 8½" wide, from muslin. Join to quilt and miter corners, as shown in Setting Diagram II. Leave corners square and trim after quilting.

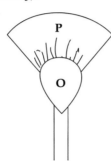

Bud Piecing Diagram

Gather 1 end of flower bud (P) under bud (O), as shown in Bud Piecing Diagram. Appliqué buds and remaining leaves (M and N) to vines, as shown. (Note that corner flowers do not have leaves [N]).

6. Make 9 yards of 1⅜"-wide continuous bias strip from print. Prepare strip as above in step 5 but use ½" bias bar. Center over seam line of inner quilt and border and appliqué.

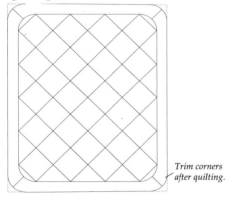

Trim corners after quilting.

Setting Diagram II

5. Cut 8 bias strips, ⅞" x 30", from green print for vines. With right sides facing and raw edges aligned, stitch edges together lengthwise using ⅛" seam allowance. Use ¼" bias bar and steam-press strips with seam centered on back. (Follow manufacturer's instructions for using bias bars, contained in packaging.) Pin vines on border, as shown in quilt photograph, and appliqué in place.

Cut 4 short bias strips, ⅞" wide, for side flowers. (See quilt photograph.) Prepare strips as above.

Quilting
Quilt in-the-ditch of seam lines of each unit. Outline-quilt ¼" inside seam lines of piece As. Quilt feathers in muslin pieces (G). Outline-quilt outside seam lines of all appliqué pieces and print border strip. Background-quilt diagonal lines, 1⅜" apart, in border.

Finished Edges
Use template G to mark border for round corners. Join print bias binding to quilt, stitching on line for round corners. Trim excess fabric from corners, leaving ¼" seam allowance. Blindstitch binding to back.

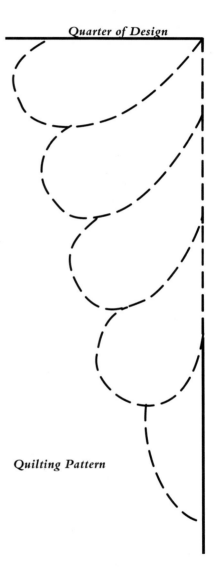

Quarter of Design

Quilting Pattern

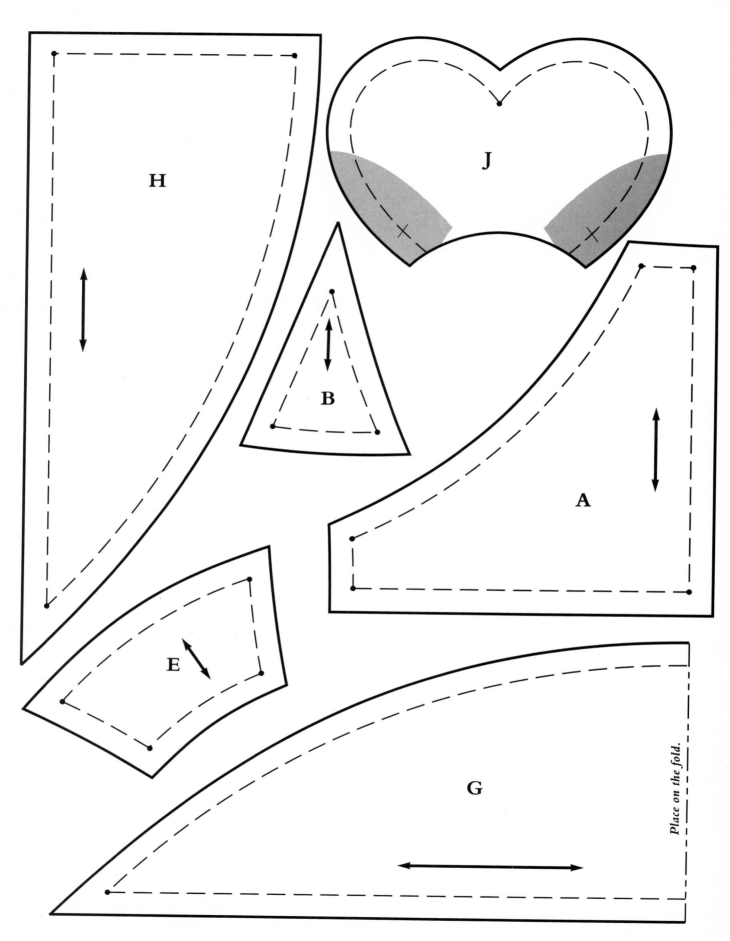

H

J

B

A

E

G

Place on the fold.

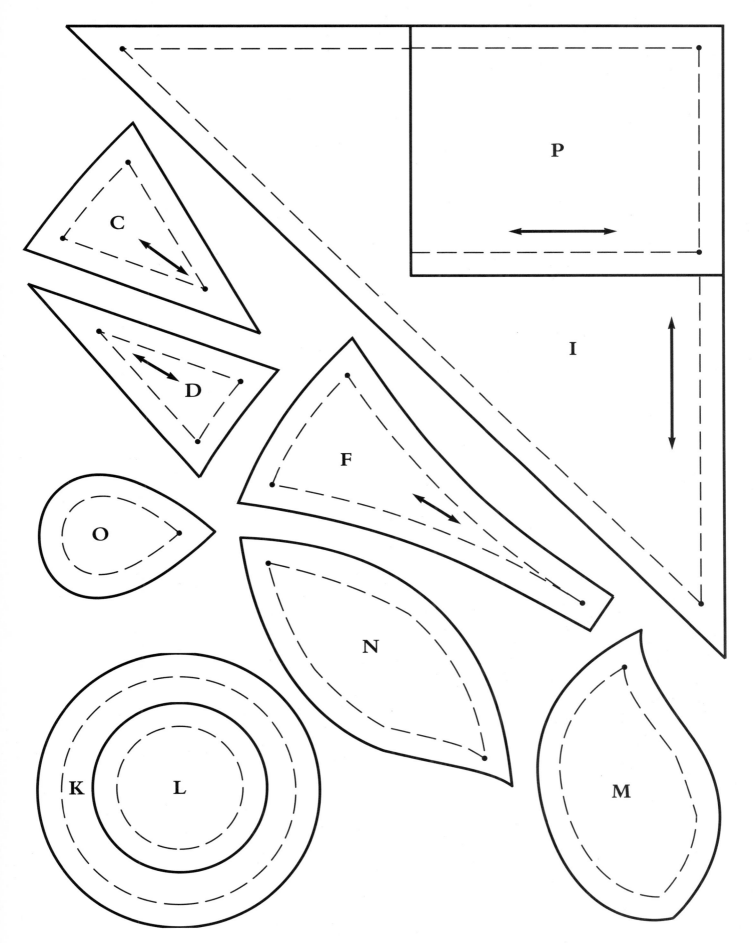

Carol Wight Jones

North Attleboro, Massachusetts

Sometimes we never know what influence we may have in another person's life. By steadily making utility quilts, Carol's Aunt Elsie played an important role in Carol's love for quilting. "She was my mentor," says Carol. "As a young girl, I would watch her make quilts, and it made me believe that I could make one, too." At age 17, Carol attempted her first quilt, cutting squares and triangles from scraps. "It took several years to complete because of high school, college, and marriage," she says, "but I enjoyed it enough to try another." Carol still uses her first quilt on her bed, and in the last 10 years she has made more than 20 quilts.

As a former guild president, Carol encourages everyone to get involved in a guild. Prior to becoming a guild member, Carol was a self-taught quilter, using methods from books and magazines. "As a guild member, I was able to participate in workshops," says Carol, "and as a result, my quilting skills have improved immensely."

Joel's Bachelor's Puzzle
1990

Joel is Carol's son, who was 12 years old when he chose the Bachelor's Puzzle block for his quilt. Says Carol, "I really was not too thrilled with the design, until he drew it on graph paper and colored it just the way he wanted it. It was beautiful. I couldn't believe it was the same design."

Several months after completing the quilt, Carol entered it in the Western Washington State Fair at Puyallup, Washington, and it was awarded a third place ribbon. (Carol lived in Fox Island, Washington, at that time.) Since 1990, Joel's quilt has been out of the house so often, traveling to quilt shows and publishers, that Joel has yet to have it in his room! He keeps asking Carol, "Mom, when am I going to get my quilt?!" We hope by the time this book is published, Joel's quilt is finally in his room.

There are two methods for piecing this quilt: the method below or a method using square A and triangle E. Square A replaces four triangle Ds and triangle E replaces two triangle Ds where blocks are seamed. The quilt is assembled in units with square As connecting them and triangle Es used in the same manner as setting pieces on the quilt edge. This is an advanced method, but many quilters will prefer it because of the elimination of so many seam allowances that would have to be quilted. (A pattern for triangle E is given on pattern page.)

Joel's Bachelor's Puzzle

Finished Quilt Size
72" x 88"

Number of Blocks and Finished Size
80 blocks—8" x 8"

Fabric Requirements★

Lt. green	—1¼ yd.
Green	—1¼ yd.
Dk. green	—¾ yd.
Lt. blue	—¾ yd.
Blue	—1¼ yd.
Navy	—1¼ yd.
Lt. lavender	—¾ yd.
Lavender	—1¼ yd.
Purple	—1¼ yd.
Pink	—1¼ yd.
Peach	—1¼ yd.
Red	—¾ yd.
Dk. gray	—2⅝ yd.
Dk. gray for bias binding	—1¼ yd.
Backing	—5¼ yd.

★All fabrics, except dk. gray, are pindots.

Other Materials
Gray quilting thread

Number to Cut

Template A	—80 dk. gray
Template B	—80 green
	80 navy
	80 lavender
	80 pink
Template B★★	—80 lt. green
	80 blue
	80 purple
	80 peach
Template C	—80 dk. green
	80 lt. blue
	80 lt. lavender
	80 red
Template D	—320 dk. gray

★★Flip or turn over template if fabric is one-sided.

Quilt Top Assembly
1. Note color arrangement and join pieces B, C, and D in units, as shown in Block Piecing Diagram. Make 4 units per block. Join units to center square (A), as shown. Make 80 blocks.
2. Arrange blocks in 10 rows of 8 blocks each. Join blocks at sides to form rows and join rows.
3. Cut 4 borders, 1½" wide, from dk. gray. Join to quilt and miter corners.

4. Cut across remaining pindot fabrics to make ¾"-wide strips. Join strips to make 2 pieced strips ¾" x 76" and 2 pieced strips ¾" x 92" long of each color.

Join strips lengthwise to make 4 pieced borders in following color order: lt. green, green, dk. green, lt. blue, blue, navy, lt. lavender, lavender, purple, pink, peach, red.

Join pieced borders to quilt with lt. green strip next to inner quilt and miter corners.

Quilting
Using gray quilting thread, outline-quilt ¼" inside seam lines of all block pieces. Quilt in-the-ditch in border seams.

Finished Edges
Bind with gray fabric.

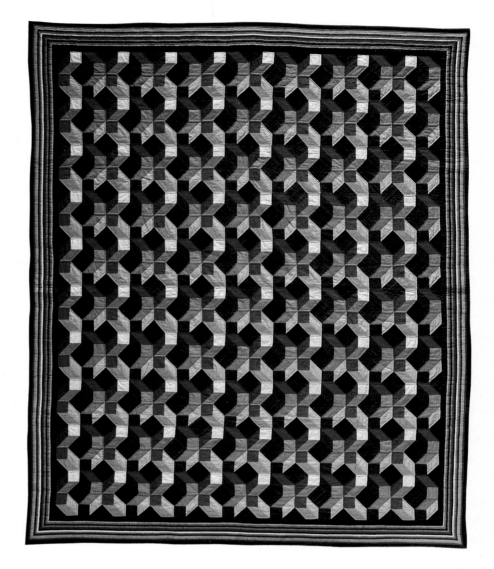

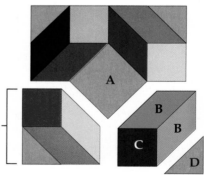

Block Piecing Diagram

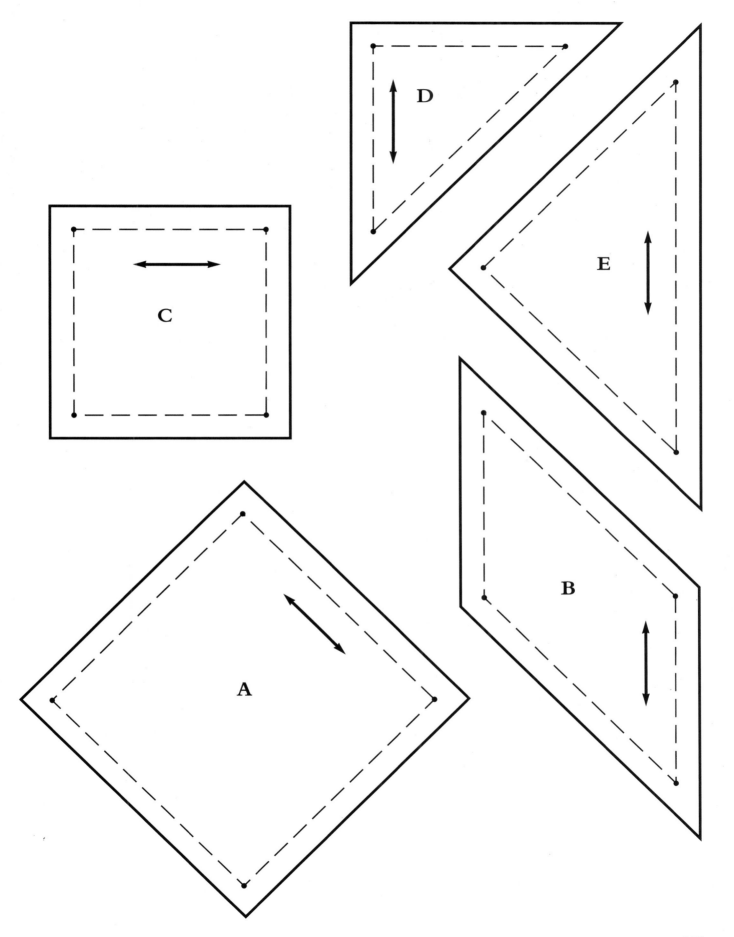

Christmas Cactus
1990

A quilted Christmas cactus is a welcome display during the Christmas season. But you'll probably find as we did that this sprightly pattern will make a cheerful addition to your home all year long.

A person who is skilled in several needlearts, as well as in oil painting, Carol has limited time for quilting. She enjoys making wall hangings since they are less time-consuming than a quilt. She thinks that you will enjoy a small project, too!

Christmas Cactus

Finished Quilt Size
38" x 38"

Number of Blocks and Finished Size
4 blocks—14" x 14"

Fabric Requirements
Muslin, bleached	—1⅛ yd.
Green print	—1⅛ yd.
Red	—1⅓ yd.
Green for bias binding	—1 yd.
Backing	—1⅜ yd.

Number to Cut
Template A	—32 red
Template B	—64 red

Other Materials
Freezer paper
Green quilting thread

Quilt Top Assembly
1. Cut four 15" squares from muslin and set aside.
2. Cut four 12½" squares from green print. Fold fabric squares in half twice and finger-press to form guidelines.
3. Cut four 12½" squares of freezer paper. Fold each square in fourths

with dull side of freezer paper on outside. (See Cactus Placement Diagram.) Lay cactus template on folded paper, as shown, and mark complete cactus pattern without seam allowance on freezer paper. Cut out pattern. Make 4.
4. Center freezer-paper pattern, with coated-side down, on right side of green print. Using a dry iron set at wool, press patterns to fabric squares.
5. Center appliqué fabric square atop 15" muslin square and pin. Start at any section of cactus and carefully cut appliqué fabric approximately ⅛"

from paper edge for seam allowance. (Cut only 2" to 3" sections at a time.)

Turn seam allowance under, even with paper edge, and appliqué to muslin square. Repeat for each muslin square.
6. Appliqué cactus blossoms (A and B) to square, as shown in block photograph. Square up and trim appliquéd blocks to 14½" x 14½".
7. Cut 8 strips for sashing, 1½" x 14½", from green print. Join to opposite sides of each block. Cut 8 strips for sashing, 1½" x 16½", from green print. Join to remaining sides.

8. Cut 2 strips for sashing, 2½" x 16½", from red. Place sashing between 2 blocks and join at sides to form a row. Make 2 rows.

Cut 1 strip for sashing, 2½" x 34½", from red. Place sashing between rows and join. (See quilt photograph.)

9. Cut 4 borders, 2½" x 39", from red. Join to quilt and miter corners. Trim excess border fabric.

Quilting

Using green quilting thread, quilt a vein down the center of each large cactus leaf.

Echo-quilt cactus design, beginning ¼" from seam line and extending out to block seam lines. Quilting lines are ¼" apart. Quilt a diagonal ½" cross-hatching pattern on rest of quilt.

Finished Edges

Bind with green fabric.

Dull Side of Freezer Paper

Cactus Placement Diagram

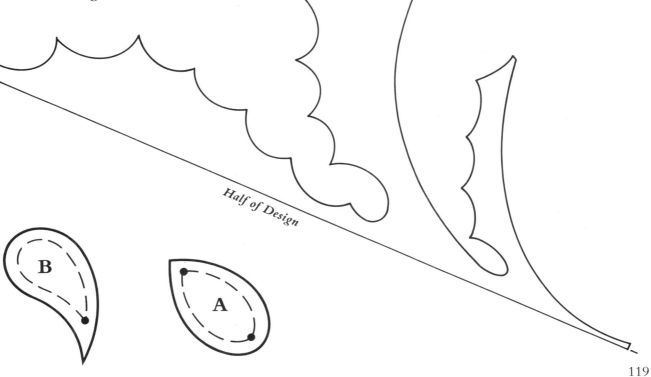

Half of Design

B

A

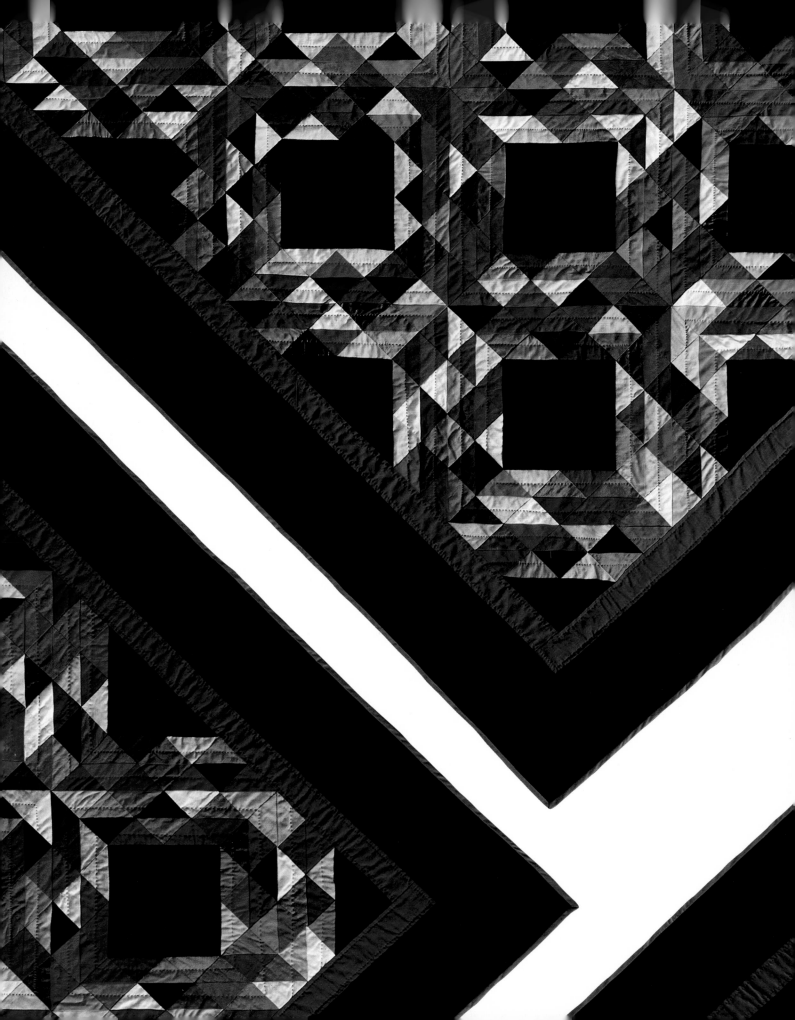

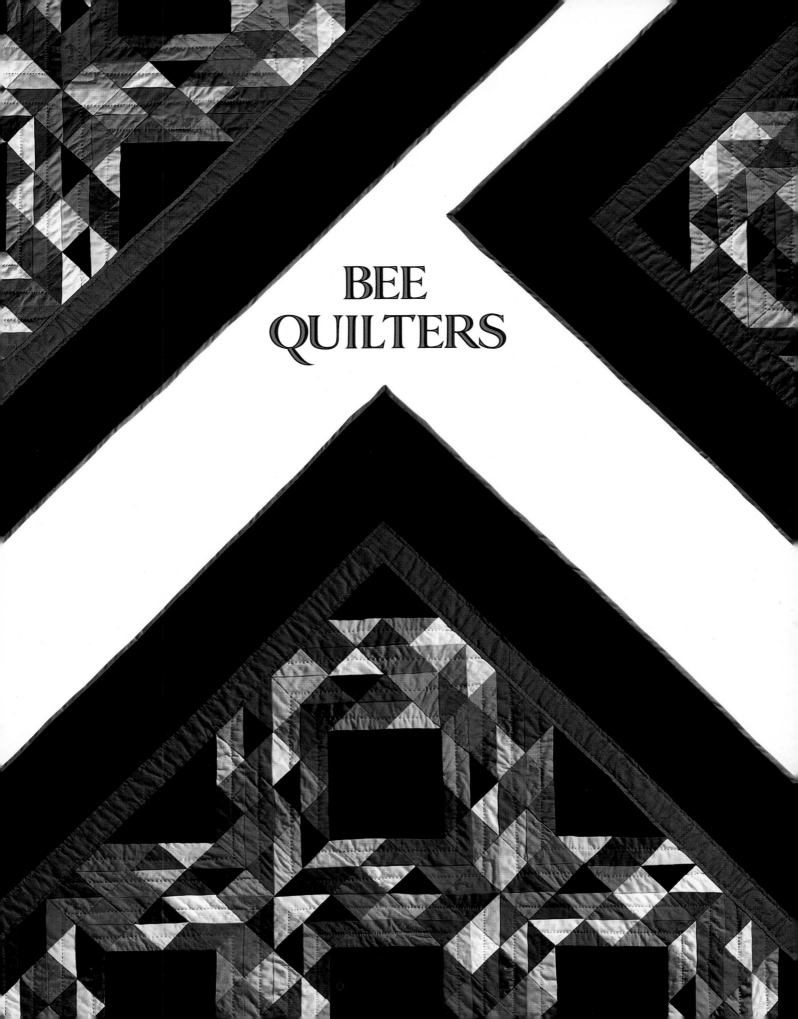

BEE
QUILTERS

Enjoying an afternoon of quilting are Ladies of the Lakes Quilt Guild members: (seated, left to right) Dot Smylie, Elaine Bassett, and Linda Thomas, and (standing, left to right) Pat Zimmerman, Kate Schaffer, Karen Miller, Kathy Michelson, Bea Sokol, Darlene Neumann, and Shirley Ahlborn.

Ladies of the Lakes Quilt Guild

Hazelhurst, Wisconsin

The Ladies of the Lakes Quilt Guild have a program they call a continual show and tell. Each member is assigned a month in which she may design her own quilt and have members help her with the piecing. "This gives each of us a good start," says guild member Karen Miller, "and encourages us to complete our quilts."

The guild has what you might call a "swinging door" membership. "Since the guild is located in a resort area," says Karen, "we have many members who are only present in the summer. Another member is present only in the winter when her family moves south from Alaska!"

For this guild, quilting is the constant that sustains their friendships even when they are apart.

Minocqua Pine Tree Centennial Quilt
1988

"Each member of our guild has special feelings for this quilt," says Karen Miller. The specialness derives from the fact that each member knows she could never have made this quilt without the encouragement of the others. The quilt-as-you-go method was used, but instructions are given here for frame quilting.

The quilt was made as a fund raiser for the Minocqua Museum and to celebrate the 100th birthday of Minocqua, Wisconsin. Makers of the quilt are: Shirley Ahlborn, Elaine Bassett, Gladys Bauers, Barbara Bennetts, Paisley Clark, Dorothy Eggie, Mary Franken, Phyllis Hardy, Pat Hruby, Lora Janak, Gail Michelson, Kathy Michelson, Karen Miller, Darlene Neumann, Kate Schaffer, Dot Smylie, Bea Sokol, Margret Stader, Bev Tabbert, Linda Thomas, and Pat Zimmerman.

Minocqua Pine Tree Centennial Quilt

Finished Quilt Size
89⅝" x 108⅞"

Number of Blocks and Finished Size
12 blocks—13⅛" x 13⅛"

Fabric Requirements

Blue print	—1½ yd.
Blue	—2 yd.
Rust	—2½ yd.
Muslin	—7½ yd.
Blue for bias binding	—1½ yd.
Backing	—9½ yd.

Number to Cut

Template A	—24 muslin
Template B	—12 muslin
	12 blue print
Template C	—12 blue print
Template D	—4 blue
Template E	—4 muslin
Template F	—28 blue
Template G	—28 muslin
13⅝" square	—6 muslin
14" square	—5 muslin
14⅜" square	—1 muslin
14½" square	—7 muslin
14" x 24" rectangle	—3 muslin
	—3 blue print
18" x 28" rectangle	—1 muslin
	—1 blue

Quilt Top Assembly

1. To make triangle-squares for Pine Tree blocks, pair 14" x 24" muslin rectangles with blue print rectangles. With right sides facing and raw edges aligned, lay muslin rectangle on top of blue print rectangle. Mark a grid of 3⅜" squares on muslin, as shown in Triangle-Squares Piecing Diagram.

Draw a diagonal line through each square, as shown.

longest line possible without cutting threads, for first "circuit" of stitching, begin at corner marked **1** on diagram and follow arrows. When you reach a fabric edge (see area marked with an X), turn fabric, but stitch "on the air" without cutting threads and continue

stitching in new direction. Start second "circuit" of stitching at point marked **2**.

Cut along marked lines to make 56 triangle-squares per rectangle. Make 168 triangle-squares.

2. Join 14 triangle-squares with

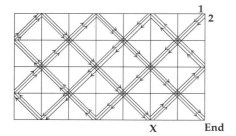

Triangle-Square Piecing Diagram

Machine-stitch ¼" on each side of diagonal lines. In order to stitch the

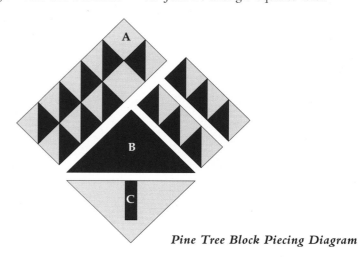

Pine Tree Block Piecing Diagram

squares (A), as shown in Pine Tree Block Piecing Diagram.

Center and appliqué tree trunk (C) to triangle (B), as shown. Join pieces to complete Pine Tree block. Make 12 blocks.

3. Cut 14" muslin squares in half on the diagonal to make 10 setting triangles. Cut 14³⁄₈" muslin square in quarters on the diagonal to make 4 corner triangles.

Join blocks (PT), setting squares (13⁵⁄₈" muslin squares), and setting

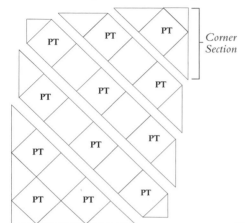

Setting Diagram I

triangles in diagonal rows, as shown in Setting Diagram I. Make 2 corner sections, as shown.

Join rows and corner sections to complete inner quilt.

4. Cut 2 border strips, 1½" wide, from rust and join to quilt sides. Cut 2 border strips, 1¹³⁄₁₆" wide, from rust and join to top and bottom of quilt.

5. Cut 14½" muslin squares in half on the diagonal to make 14 border triangles.

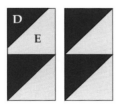

Setting Diagram II

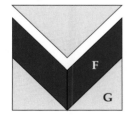

Border Section Piecing Diagram

Join border triangles and pieces F and G to make border sections, as shown in Border Section Piecing Diagram. Make 14 sections. Set aside.

6. Make 12 triangle-squares from 18" x 28" muslin and blue rectangles,

using grid method in step 1. Mark a grid of 8⁷⁄₈" squares.

Join 3 triangle-squares with pieces D and E, as shown in Border Corner

Border Corner Block Piecing Diagram

Block Piecing Diagram. Make 4 blocks.

7. Join 4 border sections to form border for quilt side, as shown in Setting Diagram II. Make 2 and join to quilt.

Join remaining border sections in 2 groups of 3 sections each for top and bottom borders. Join border corner

blocks to each end and join to quilt.

Quilting
Outline-quilt ¼" inside seam lines of muslin triangles in Pine Tree blocks. Quilt heart-flower quatrefoil in each setting square and border corner block. Quilt half heart-flower quatrefoil in setting triangles and border triangles. Quilt 3 parallel lines, 1" apart, down the center of zigzag blue border pieces.

Finished Edges
Bind with blue fabric.

125

Quarter of Design

**Heart-Flower Quatrefoil
Quilting Pattern
(See below left for
reduced completed design.)**

*Shaded portion indicates
overlap from following page.*

126

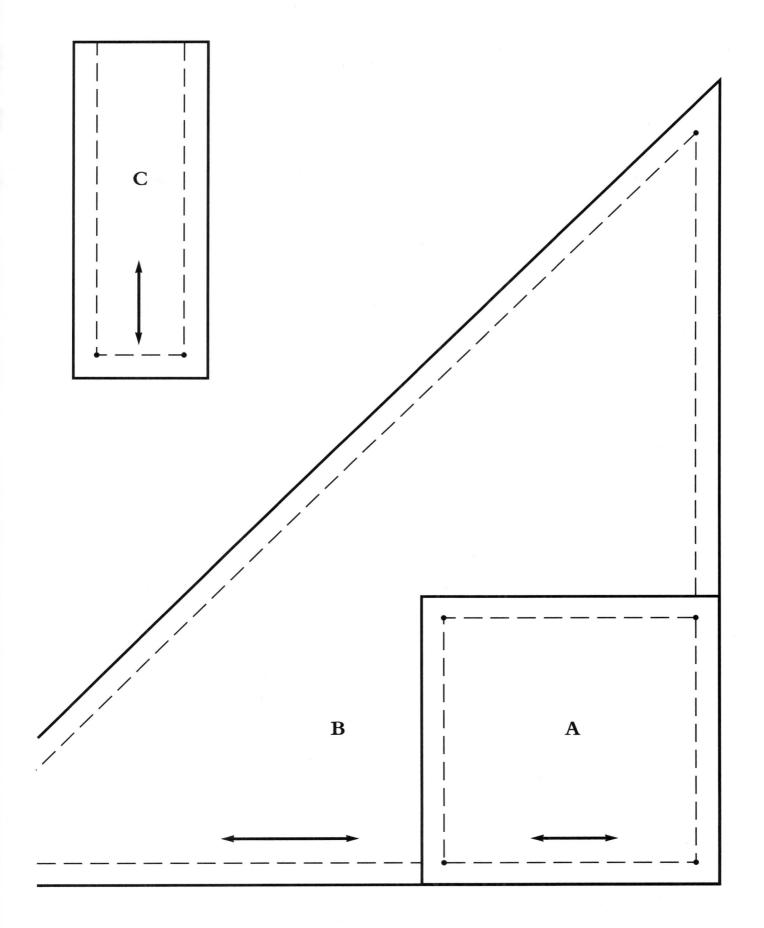

C

B

A

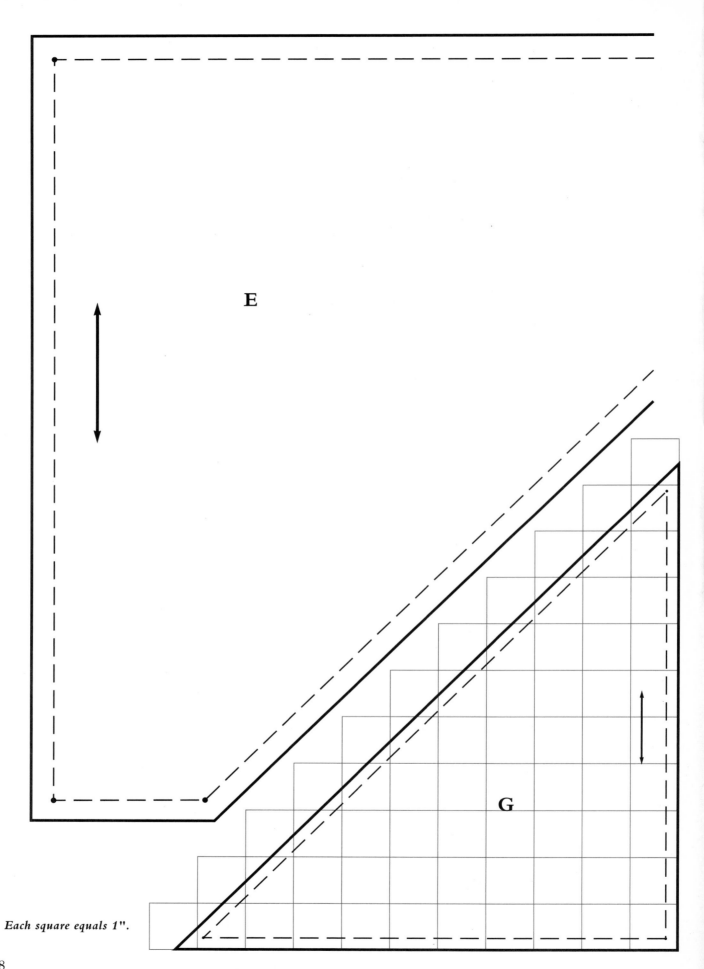

Each square equals 1".

E

G

Shaded portion indicates overlap from preceding page.
Each square equals 1".
F
D

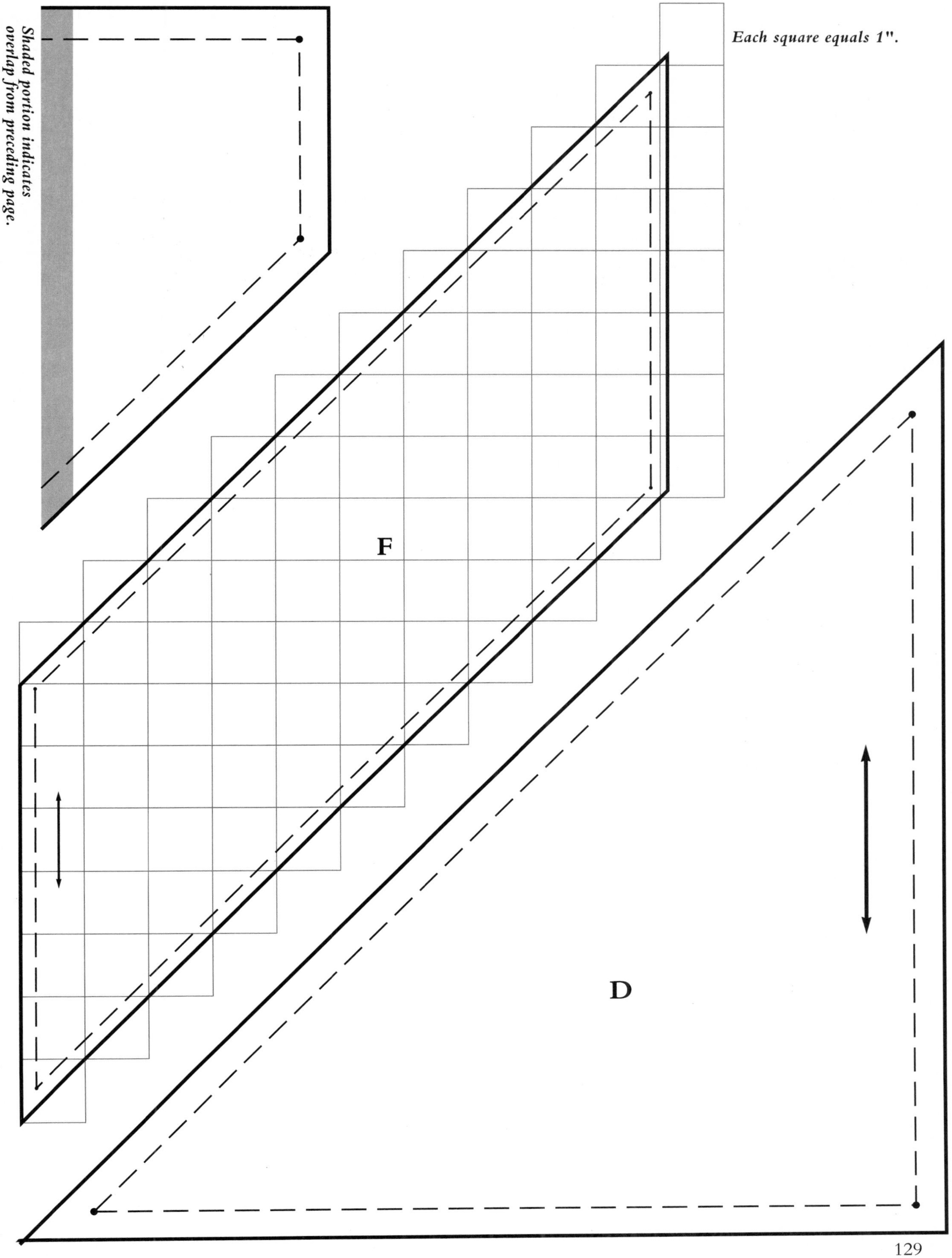

Six members of the Narrows Connection Quiltmakers are: (seated, left to right) Janet Lockhart, Lynda Kelley, and Janice Elliott, and (standing, left to right) Helen Newlands, Ginny Sands, and Jessie Richardson.

Narrows Connection Quiltmakers

Gig Harbor and Tacoma, Washington

Each spring members of the Narrows Connection Quiltmakers eagerly look forward to their quilting retreat. "No programs are planned," says former president Carol Jones. "It's a time to get away and to work intensely on our own projects."

Besides making doll quilts for needy children each Christmas, members make one group quilt each year. Each member gets one chance to win the quilt for every hour that she works on the quilt. The drawing for the quilt is usually held in December; that way, the winner gets a new quilt for Christmas!

The Narrows Connection Quiltmakers was formed in 1982, and their annual show is held in the spring at the Fox Island Historical Museum.

Ocean Waves
1987

This Amish-style *Ocean Waves* quilt continues be a favorite among quilters. This is one of the group quilts members made for their drawing at the end of the year (described above). Members quick-pieced triangle-squares and held work parties to assemble and baste the quilt. It was circulated among individual members for quilting. Those members who worked so diligently on *Ocean Waves* were: Diane Armstrong, Terry Bader, Virginia Carter, Linda Davis, Julie Desseau, Willie Dowling, Janice Elliott, Kathy Fina, Martha Gruber, Nancy Johnson, Carol Jones, Karen Jung, Lynda Kelley, Janet Lockhart, Gayle Loesch, Esther Marlatt, Kathy Miner, Harriet Mooney, Julie Munkres, Helen Newlands, Ginger Paddock, Janice Richards, Jessie Richardson, Ginny Sands, and Sue Williams.

Ocean Waves

Finished Quilt Size
Approximately 75½" x 95½"

Number of Blocks and Finished Size
18 blocks—approx. 21¼" x 21¼"

Fabric Requirements
Solids★ —5¾ yd. total
Teal —2½ yd.
Black —2¾ yd.
Rose for bias
 binding —1¼ yd.
Backing —5¾ yd.

★Include a few polished cottons to imitate the sparkle of the ocean. A 11" x 17" rectangle from 2 contrasting solids is needed to make 30 triangle-squares. You will be making 288 triangle-squares. (See step 1.)

Other Materials
Black quilting thread

Number to Cut
Triangle —576 solids

Quilt Top Assembly
1. Cut twenty 11" x 17" rectangles from solids. Pair rectangles with contrasting colors and lay one rectangle on top of the other, with right sides facing and aligning raw edges. Mark a grid of 3⅜" squares on top fabric, as shown in Triangle-Squares Piecing Diagram. Draw a diagonal line

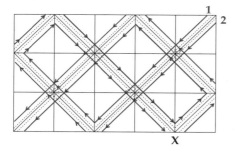

Triangle-Square Piecing Diagram

through each square, as shown.

Machine-stitch ¼" on each side of diagonal lines. In order to stitch the longest line without cutting threads, for first "circuit" of stitching, begin at corner marked 1 on diagram and follow arrows. When you reach a fabric edge (see area marked with an X), turn fabric, but stitch "on the air" without cutting threads and continue stitching in new direction. Start second "circuit" of stitching at point

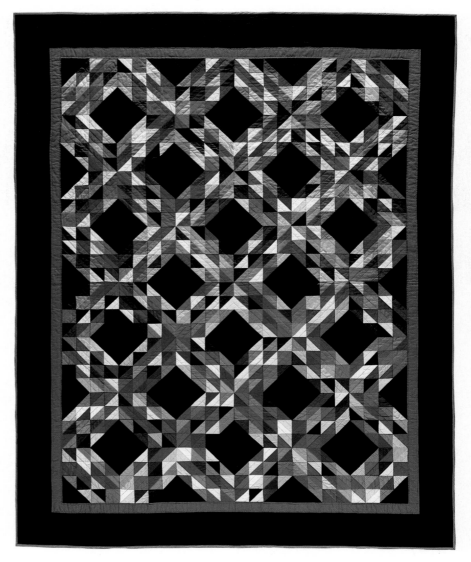

marked 2. Cut along marked lines to make 30 triangle-squares for each rectangle. Make 288 triangle-squares.

2. Set aside a 28" x 86" rectangle of black for borders. Cut eighteen 7½" squares, five 7⅞" squares, and one 8¼" square from black.

Cut 7⅞" squares in half on the diagonal to make 10 triangles. Cut 8¼" square in quarters on the diagonal to make 4 corner triangles.

3. The Narrows Connection Quiltmakers arranged all pieces of the inner quilt on a wall before sewing them together to obtain the best color movement. Arrange pieces in blocks, setting triangles, and corner triangles, as shown in respective piecing diagrams and Setting Diagram.

When you are satisfied with the color arrangement, join triangle-squares, triangles, and 7½" squares to make 18 blocks, as shown in Block Piecing Diagram. Make 10 setting triangles, as shown in Setting Triangle Piecing Diagram. Make 4 corner triangles, as shown in Corner Triangle Piecing Diagram.

4. Join blocks and setting triangles in diagonal rows, as shown in Setting Diagram. Make 2 corner sections, as shown.

Join rows and corner sections to complete inner quilt.

5. Cut 2 borders, 2½" wide, from teal and join to sides of quilt. Cut 2 borders, 2½" wide, from teal and join to top and bottom of quilt.

6. Cut 2 borders, 6½" wide, from black and join to sides of quilt. Cut 2 borders, 6½" wide, from black and join to top and bottom of quilt.

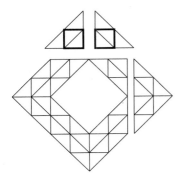

Block Piecing Diagram

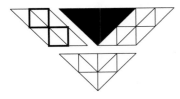

Setting Triangle Piecing Diagram

Corners Triangle Piecing Diagram

Quilting

Quilt your favorite pattern in the center of each black square. Quilt across triangles, as shown in Block Quilting Diagram. Continue straight-line quilting for setting and corner triangles.

Outline-quilt ¼" inside seam lines of teal borders. In black borders, quilt

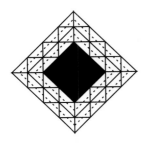

Block Quilting Diagram

diagonal lines, running from right-hand corner to left-hand corner of quilt, 2" apart.

Finished Edges

Bind with rose fabric.

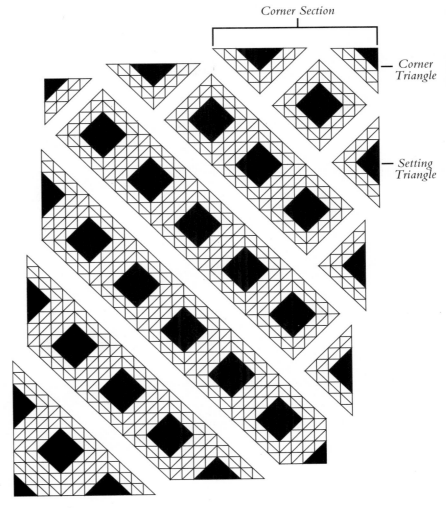

Corner Section

Corner Triangle

Setting Triangle

Setting Diagram

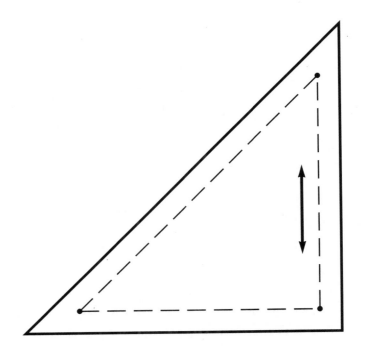

DESIGNER GALLERY

Fifteen of the 55 makers of Stitchville *are (seated left to right)—Fran Peters, Cleo Benson, Ann Vidmar, Eldora Brown, Hilda Sooter, and (standing, left to right)—Mary Levy, Eleanor Leftwich, Dorothy Archer, Ruth McCoy, Glynda Kozak, Cynthia Forrest, Henriette Mensonides, Bev Weeks, Arline Dolliver, and Jeri Schellhous.*

El Camino Quilters

Carlsbad, California

Since 1980, El Camino Quilters have maintained their commitment to be involved with the charities in their community. Quilts are made each year for groups such as nursing homes, homes for battered women and children, and the Ronald McDonald house, to name a few. The guild's 80 members meet twice a month to upgrade their skills at workshops and to hear lectures by outstanding professional quilters. The third Tuesday of each month is designated as basting day, when members set aside time to baste the guild's quilts, and maybe a few of their own.

Stitchville
1990

The El Camino Quilters took a step away from their traditional sampler quilt project and walked right into *Stitchville*. *Stitchville* is the brainchild of member Arline Dolliver. At the time of *Stitchville*'s development, she was affectionately known by members as the town planner since she set up the "architectural" guidelines and coordinated all block designs. The only restriction was that the same blue fabric be used for the sky in each block.

Members were encouraged to be as creative as they wanted to be, and that's what made it fun. If you'll look closely, you'll find embroidered chickens in a barnyard, a horse and buggy, detachable quilts on a clothesline, a tire swing, and flowerpots on windowsills.

A sashing of gray or brown was placed between each row of blocks to represent the streets, and extra trees and foliage were added after the blocks were assembled. Why, of course, isn't that what the paving contractors and landscapers do after a neighborhood is built?

"If you have the ability to design," says Cecily, "I believe it is a God-given gift that you must use to its fullest for the pleasure and benefit of others, and thereby yourself. This is a responsibility that I feel must be carried out." Cecily acts upon her belief by spending her days and nights designing quilts, needlepoint, rag dolls, and knitting projects. She also stencils and does freehand paintings on walls and floors.

Following her philosophy, in 1981, Cecily initiated a support group for women whose husbands had terminal cancer. She taught the women to quilt and continues to oversee their activities, in addition to working with two other similar groups weekly.

Yes, her quilts and designs have won awards, but more important to her is the time she spends sharing her gift with others.

Cecily H. Zerega
Fairfield, Connecticut

Barns
1984
The beauty of this quilt is in its simplicity. A group of barns is interspersed with trees in a network of pristine lines.

Turn this book upside down to appreciate even more Cecily's handling of the watery reflection. Solid polished cotton pieces duplicate the shimmering reflection of the pond.

Since Cecily and her daughter, Libby, share a love of old barns, Cecily made this quilt for her.

This modest man devoted most of his life to teaching young people in the field of office occupations. When he retired, he spent his time maintaining two greenhouses, both an iris and daylily garden, and also doing a little woodworking on the side. That took care of Pete's daytime hours, but he wanted something to do in those long winter evenings. That's when quilting entered his life.

"I wanted a challenge," he says, "and I found it in quilting. I was too embarrassed to seek help by taking classes, so I learned by trial and error." As his quiltmaking progressed, Pete broadened his horizons by attending quilt shows and demonstrations. In 1989, he joined a guild. "My wife, Jane, attends with me," says Pete, "but she goes only to support me; she does not quilt."

Pete has made more than 12 quilts and now prefers developing his own designs, usually around a theme.

Pete James B. Johnson

Fort Worth, Texas

Glimmer of Hope
1990

Glimmer of Hope symbolizes Pete's love for his homeland, America, and his Indian heritage. Pete's symbolism begins with the center row of diamonds. The yellow represents the peaceful harmony that Indian tribes experienced before the white man came. The reds represent the blood that was shed during the fierce battles between the white man and the Indian.

The black on the outer edge of the diamonds symbolizes the elimination of many Indians and how those who survived were herded onto reservations. The turquoise represents the U.S. Cavalry, and the following row of white, the false peace between them. The red and black between the white represents the renegades who escaped the reservations. The last row of white represents a more-or-less stable peace.

The top and bottom rows represent Pete's frustration and lack of hope for the future. "What does it hold for our grandchildren," he asks, "because man has done much to destroy this Earth so far?" To represent a mere glimmer of hope for the future, Pete placed one yellow rectangle on the binding. "We mustn't let the light go out," says Pete.

Haunted Mesas
1990

When Pete learned that he was of Cherokee Indian ancestry, he decided to make and design quilts with Indian themes. He was inspired to make *Haunted Mesas* after reading Louis L'Amour's novel by a similar name. Pete took the design from a traditional Sioux Indian bead design.

Haunted Mesas has a total of 8,475 small rectangles. The quilt measures 106 inches square and is machine-pieced and handquilted. "Never again!" says Pete. "But, since this quilt was for my grandson, it was less of a chore."

MACHINE PIECED HAND QUILTED
BY PETE JOHNSON 1989-90
MY GRAND SON BENJAMIN HARRIS
JOHNSON I AM SO PROUD OF YOU
BEN LOVE GRAND DADDY

Rosemarie Stanley
Marietta, Georgia

When Rosemarie moved from Chicago to Marietta, Georgia, the first thing she did was to locate and join the nearest quilt guild. "I have always found quilters to be friendly, generous, and encouraging people," she says, "and I knew that by joining a guild I would be involved with individuals who shared my interests."

Quilting keeps Rosemarie physically and mentally busy and challenged. She starts each quilt with only an idea and a little fabric. "I seldom plan a quilt," she says. "I find it too restricting, and I lose interest in it. By improvising as I go, I never know what the final result will be, and it's more fun that way."

Pride of the Carousel
1990

"I have always liked carousel horses," says Rosemarie. "When my husband made one in stained glass, I revised his pattern and designed a wall hanging in Christmas colors and fabrics."

Studded with beads, sequins, and gold braid, Rosemarie's prancing horse was contoured by being stuffed and appliquéd. Lines of back-stitching in black add details to the horse's mane and head.

Small fabric leaf cutouts decorate his saddle. The leaves are glued in an overlapping design, accented with pearl and green beading. Rosemarie chose to background-quilt heavily to flatten the background even more and make the horse more prominent. Gold braid is stitched to the border seam lines and quilt edges.

"Many people have told me that this quilt isn't just for Christmas," says Rosemarie, "so it has a place to hang all year long."

As a native of the Southwest, Katy tells us that she needs to look no further than the Western sky for endless inspiration for quilt designs. "Its people and their cultures are my constant inspiration," says Katy. Four generations of Katy's family have lived in New Mexico, and though she has lived in many other places, she finds that New Mexico is the most beautiful.

Katy's grandmothers were pioneers and quilters who left a legacy for her to follow. "I cherish the quilts they made," says Katy, "and I look at my quiltmaking as a way to honor them and a way to continue the tradition of this art."

Katy J. Widger
Los Lunas, New Mexico

Los Lentes Twilight
1990

A summer sunset in New Mexico is like no other, according to Katy. "Before I made *Los Lentes Twilight*, I stared at the sky in awe and wonder until the last glimmer of color had faded and the stars were shining through," says Katy. "Then I went into the house and started figuring my fabric dye formulas."

Katy chose Variable-Star-Within-a-Variable-Star blocks and integrated them with a flowing sequence of colors to replicate the transformation of the sky from daylight to dark. By hand-dyeing fabrics in a 20-step color gradation from yellow to magenta, Katy ensured that no two pieces of any one star were the same exact color.

Each day is filled with some sort of quilting activity for Rita. She is an instructor, lecturer, and published writer on all types of quilt-making techniques. The demands on her time are numerous, but this former artist makes it a point to set aside plenty of time to work on her own projects. As you can see from the quilts shown below, Rita is accomplished in the art of appliqué and embroidery. Her attention to detail makes her quilts both outstanding and one-of-a-kind.

Rita Denenberg
Royal Palm Beach, Florida

Osceola, Indian Warrior
1987

After moving to Florida from New York, Rita and her husband toured southern Florida, gleaning bits of Florida history along the way. Encouraged by her tour guide, Rita spent time in the library poring over books about the Seminoles, who settled that area. "It was Osceola who touched my heart," she says, "with his love of Florida, which I share." Rita was especially moved by the suffering Osceola endured at the hands of his oppressors (the U.S. Government) and felt that making him the subject of a quilt would be a fitting tribute. "It gives me the opportunity to educate others about his bravery and passion for his beloved Seminole tribe," says Rita.

Rita layer-appliquéd Osceola, using an Indian print fabric for his shawl and headdress. His beaded necklace is made from individually stuffed appliquéd circles. The fringe that hangs from his shawl and sash is made from single strands of embroidery floss. The Osceola quilt is appropriately bordered with Seminole patchwork.

The Magic Flute
1989

Rita exhibits her expertise as a fabric artist and needleworker with this extraordinary quilt. Tiny buttonhole stitches, applied by hand, anchor cutout flowers to the kimono and the border. Beads embellish gold hair combs, and precise placement of quilting lines replicate the motion of disturbed water. The magic in the title refers to the fact that when the Japanese lady plays her flute, a carp leaps out of the water to greet her.

Rita developed this design because she wanted to make a quilt with *broderie perse* detailing. She spent four months, including traveling to several states, looking for just the right floral chintz, "only to find it in a local shop!" she says. Though Rita spent two years overall on this project, her efforts were rewarded when *The Magic Flute* received the second place ribbon in the appliqué professional category at the 1990 American Quilter's Society Show.

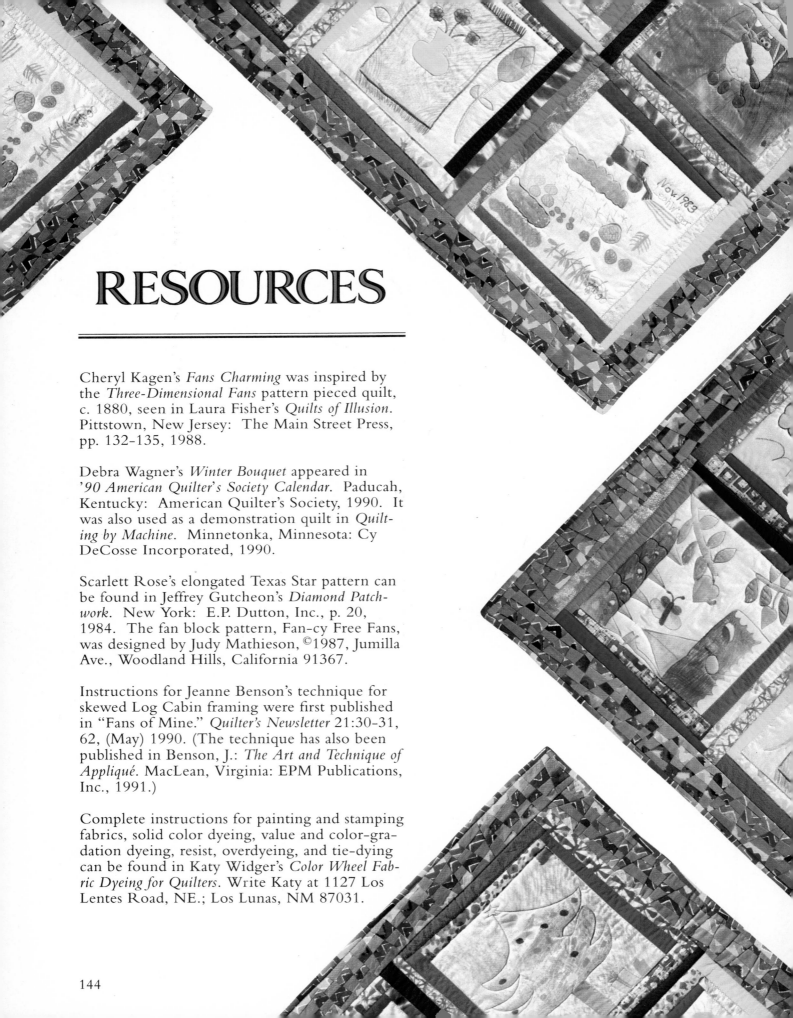

RESOURCES

Cheryl Kagen's *Fans Charming* was inspired by the *Three-Dimensional Fans* pattern pieced quilt, c. 1880, seen in Laura Fisher's *Quilts of Illusion*. Pittstown, New Jersey: The Main Street Press, pp. 132–135, 1988.

Debra Wagner's *Winter Bouquet* appeared in *'90 American Quilter's Society Calendar*. Paducah, Kentucky: American Quilter's Society, 1990. It was also used as a demonstration quilt in *Quilting by Machine*. Minnetonka, Minnesota: Cy DeCosse Incorporated, 1990.

Scarlett Rose's elongated Texas Star pattern can be found in Jeffrey Gutcheon's *Diamond Patchwork*. New York: E.P. Dutton, Inc., p. 20, 1984. The fan block pattern, Fan-cy Free Fans, was designed by Judy Mathieson, ©1987, Jumilla Ave., Woodland Hills, California 91367.

Instructions for Jeanne Benson's technique for skewed Log Cabin framing were first published in "Fans of Mine." *Quilter's Newsletter* 21:30–31, 62, (May) 1990. (The technique has also been published in Benson, J.: *The Art and Technique of Appliqué*. MacLean, Virginia: EPM Publications, Inc., 1991.)

Complete instructions for painting and stamping fabrics, solid color dyeing, value and color-gradation dyeing, resist, overdyeing, and tie-dying can be found in Katy Widger's *Color Wheel Fabric Dyeing for Quilters*. Write Katy at 1127 Los Lentes Road, NE.; Los Lunas, NM 87031.